8.15.98

Julie,

Our God is faithful!

Connie Neal

In Praise of
Dancing in the Arms of God

Though written for women, this is a book everyone needs to read. When you read Connie Neal's work, she gives you a window, not only into her heart, but into the heart of God as well.

David Stoop, Ph.D.
Author, *Making Peace with Your Father*

Dancing in the Arms of God will encourage you, regardless of your situation in life. Connie Neal tells her story with an open heart as she reveals God's faithfulness in times when happiness and personal fulfillment seem the most remote. Comforting reassurance for the hurting.

Zig Ziglar

Connie Neal's book sings with word pictures and stories that reach deep into the heart. As I read, I hear the melody and I, too, want to dance with God. A must reading for anyone who longs for intimacy with the Divine.

Rachael Crabb

Every woman longs for a "handsome prince" to rescue and transform her. In *Dancing in the Arms of God* Connie Neal captures the draw of Cinderella and shows us all how to claim our own happy ending through our Prince of Peace—Jesus Christ.

Florence Littauer
President, CLASS Speakers, Inc.
Author, *Silver Boxes* and *I've Found My Keys, Now Where's My Car?*

Dancing in the Arms of God

Finding intimacy and fulfillment by following his lead

CONNIE NEAL

ZondervanPublishingHouse
Grand Rapids, Michigan

A Division of HarperCollins*Publishers*

Dancing in the Arms of God
Copyright © 1995 by Connie Neal

Discussion Guide copyright © 1997 by Connie Neal

Requests for information should be addressed to:

≝ ZondervanPublishingHouse
Grand Rapids, Michigan 49530

Library of Congress Cataloging-in-Publication Data

Neal, C. W. (Connie W.), 1958–
    Dancing in the arms of God : finding intimacy and fulfillment by following His
lead / Connie Neal.
        p.   cm.
    ISBN: 0-310-20113-6 (hardcover)
    ISBN: 0-310-21915-9 (softcover)
        1. Neal, C. W. (Connie W.), 1958–   . 2. Christian biography—United States.
I. Title.
BR1725.N38   1995
248.8'43—dc20   95-37401
                                                                                      CIP

Interior design by Sherri L. Hoffman

Published in association with Sealy M. Yates, Literary Agent, Orange, CA

Printed in the United States of America

98 99 00 01 02 03 04 /❖ DH/ 10

CONTENTS

To Patrick Neal,
Kimberly and Rick Roberts,
and
Rayna and Larry Bertolucci,
whose true love and friendship
have sustained me

Foreword

I BEGAN READING the manuscript of *Dancing in the Arms of God* while considering Connie Neal as a possible co-author for my next book. I hoped to get a sense of her writing style, but to my delight, I found so much more, including a kindred spirit.

When our relationship first began, Connie spoke honestly and openly with me. There was no pretense, she was real, and that was what drew me to her. Even though our circumstances and suffering came in different forms, the wisdom and insights we learned through our faith and hope in God were very similar.

Connie shares her spiritual pilgrimage in *Dancing in the Arms of God* with refreshing honesty, passion, and humor. Even though the book follows the allegory of the fairy tale *Cinderella*, it is a true and gutsy story of one woman's survival and search for spiritual fulfillment. Connie is not afraid to share her heartaches, disappointments and failures along the journey. She brings hope and encouragement to others through her story. You may identify with some of the problems that Connie faced, but may not have been able to openly admit them to yourself or others. I admire Connie's courage and vulnerability in an effort to help others to learn that God's truth truly can set you free.

I am reminded of C. S. Lewis' words from *Shadowlands*. "We read to know that we are not alone." This book is written to let others know that they are not alone.

I am confident you will be inspired and encouraged, as I was, as you read *Dancing in the Arms of God*.

Jan Dravecky

Prelude

The story always begins the same way: a girl dreams her dreams
even though she is degraded, unappreciated,
her beauty undiscovered, her true value maligned
by those who only see her as she appears.
The heart of the story takes place in her transformation,
brought about by the love of one who can see
beyond the surface of how she appears
or where she fits in society's pecking order.
She sits near the fireplace, sleeps among the cinders.
She dreams that someday her prince will come,
lift her up from her lowly situation,
and recognize her true beauty.
And yet, in spite of her dreams
she is disillusioned, limited by her reality.
She is still bound to slave away
and return to sit alone among the cinders.
She lives her life trying to please people,
feeling like everybody's servant, giving herself away.
She has not the freedom to care for herself
but no one else is there to care for her.
Until . . .

An invitation arrives from the palace: The Prince is giving a ball!
　　By royal decree: All the eligible maidens are to attend!
　　　　She yearns to take part in the dance,
　　　　　　but fears she may be deemed ineligible.
She can look at herself and see she's not fit to mingle with royalty.
　　Then hope appears, in the form of someone with vision
　　　　who can see beyond her cinders; someone with power
　　　　　　to transform her into the woman she is meant to be.
Dancing at the ball is everything she dared hope for and more.
　　The Prince is drawn to her, takes her in his arms, and they dance!
　　　　But she isn't surprised when the magical moment is over
　　　　　　scarcely after it began.
She is still more comfortable
　　being known as Cinderella
　　　　than as a vision of beauty,
　　　　　　dancing gracefully in the arms of the prince.
To her amazement, he can't bear to let her go.
　　He seeks after her, determined to find her
　　　　to share his kingdom with her
　　　　　　to bring out the beauty he sees within her.
Haltingly, she dares to hope in happily ever after,
　　dares to hope his love can find a way. She can see it!
But . . .
The villain steps in. Her captors bar her way.
　　She faces a locked door,
　　　　the shattering of her hopes,
　　　　　　the resurgence of old familiar doubts.
Can her faith in his love for her
　　outweigh the pain of her misfortune,
　　　　her belief in her own unworthiness?
　　　　　　She waits in hope to dance once more.

Her hope is not disappointed.
His love for her proves true.
Her sorrows give way to gladness.
Her shame is remembered no more.
In the final scene, Princess Ella is transformed entirely:
in her situation, appearance, and self-concept.
His love brought out the beauty beneath the cinders—
And they lived happily ever after!

ONE

Dancing in the Arms of God

*Finding intimacy and fulfillment
by following his lead*

Perhaps we love the Cinderella fairy tale so because it corresponds to a hope within every one of us. It captures the desire of all humanity in its promise of deliverance from bondage, its hope for a "happily ever after." And its themes speak deeply to longings hidden within us.

Some women seek fulfillment by looking inside themselves. But true fulfillment comes by looking to God, yielding to his loving embrace, and following his lead. It's not an independent effort; it's a dynamic relationship. I call it dancing in the arms of God.

Cinderella themes resonate throughout the Bible, drawing me in, stirring up hope that my hunger for intimacy and desire for personal fulfillment can be satisfied. The prophet Isaiah says that God comes to mend broken hearts and set prisoners free. He promises a crown of beauty, the oil of gladness, and a garment of praise (Isaiah 61:3). Those who have had a hopeless beginning can be freed and transformed to display God's splendor. This is the promise of God, who cannot lie.

I cherish my Cinderella aspirations in light of God's promise. Perhaps I do so because my early life mirrors the beginning of the story, and my aspirations, like Cinderella's, exceed anything I could reach without powerful help. I share my story to encourage you to rekindle *your* Cinderella aspirations—regardless of where you now find yourself.

THE BLACK AND WHITE snapshot came from a box of old family photographs. The little girl in the photo looks to be about six or seven. Her long, blond hair is parted evenly into two ponytails, each adorned with ribbons tied in pretty bows. Her bangs are shiny-clean and well-combed, and her plaid dress is smoothed into folds. The smile on her little-girl face beams brightly. But she is seated on a garbage can, amidst other garbage cans in an alley.

The photograph is a picture of me as a little girl. I don't remember who took the picture. I have no idea why they would put such a pretty little girl out with the trash. Surely that is not what they meant to do. But the picture connected with something hidden deep inside me, something I feared about myself. It seemed that, regardless of how pretty I looked or how sweetly I smiled, anyone seeing the photo would see me only in the context of the garbage surrounding me. Like Cinderella, whose beauty was originally obscured by the cinders in which she sat, I feared that the circumstances that had surrounded my life might keep me from expressing the beauty shining in that little girl's smile. I feared that, no matter how hard I worked or how much I tried, I might always live my life against the backdrop of garbage.

When that photograph was taken, I was trying hard to hold on to my hopes and dreams, even though the harsh realities of life threatened to disillusion me. My sister and I were being shuffled back and forth each week between two sets of parents: Mom and her husband, Abie, and my Dad and his wife, Edith. My mom and dad had never been married to each other. Mom drank heavily. Her husband, Abie, was dying of emphysema at the age of forty-four. Two of their five children were teenagers, still living at home, and one son was in prison. My sister and I, Mom's two youngest daughters, also lived with her and Abie during the week, staying at our dad's house on the weekends.

I was very close to my stepfather, Abie, and held a favored position in his eyes. This only made the pain of watching him slowly cough himself to death that much harder to take. I tried my best to be a good girl, desperately hoping that if I were good enough I could hold back death. But for the first time, I realized a valuable lesson: I didn't have the power to protect myself or those I loved. Abie died when I was seven.

Mom drank more regularly and grew terribly depressed, behaving erratically after Abie's death. Yet the more Mom drank, the harder I tried to please her. I couldn't help thinking that if I could make her proud enough of me, maybe she wouldn't drink anymore. For years I tried to be good enough to change those I loved. When that didn't work, I rebelled, daring anyone who cared to try to turn my life around. No one seemed to notice or care, at least not enough to do anything.

All the while, part of me was still that little girl, smiling my best, hoping someone would see me— the real me—and love me. I always had the feeling my life mattered greatly to someone out there, to whoever created me. I wanted God to come to my rescue, but I didn't know how to reach him.

I struggled through several difficult years, losing touch with the God I believed in as a child. I also lost touch with my little-girl hope that I was a special person. All hope I had of distancing myself from the pain and struggles around me began to fade, and I ventured into adolescence with a fair amount of anger because life wasn't turning out as I had wanted. I began to medicate my anger and uncertainty with alcohol and recreational drugs.

ONE COLD JANUARY NIGHT when I was fourteen, I went with a friend to a place called Calvary Chapel. We didn't go looking for God; like most girls our age, we went to meet boys. The enormous tent was filled with others like my friend and me: young people in search of a good time, drawn by word that something unusual was happening here. The young people in the crowd dressed casually, in jeans and jackets and tie-dyed skirts. Some had blankets wrapped around their shoulders to fend off the cold. Some looked like hippies—I saw a lot of long-haired boys and more than a few pairs of drug-dazed eyes. Not your typical church crowd.

The excited chatter of hundreds of people filled the air. I sensed there was more to the scene than what I could see. On stage a band played contemporary music, but with lyrics that were either about God or sung to God. The crowd clapped and cheered as each song ended. Every cold metal folding chair was filled, and those who couldn't find a chair sat on the ground near the stage and along the aisles. They swayed to the beat, laughing and smiling, some linked arm in arm; whole rows of kids were holding hands and singing loudly. It was as though we had walked into another dimension, one filled with love where no one could resist being happy. I wanted to get closer, to know what made them act this way.

After the musicians left, a young man in jeans came on stage with a Bible in his hand. He spoke as though Jesus were sitting in the chair next to me. He said Jesus loved everyone, even me, and that he valued me so much that he died for the privilege of having a love relationship with me. As a child in Sunday school I had heard the story before, but this was different. He stressed the point that Jesus was alive right now, waiting for us to decide if we wanted to know him and love him. He said Jesus proved he was God's only Son when he rose from the dead, and that he never died again. He asked us to believe that Jesus was waiting nearby, invisible but real, waiting for us to respond to his invitation.

I was captivated by the promise of such a love. If the man was telling the truth, this love was beyond any love I had dared hope for. I was ready, but for some reason the man dismissed the meeting without telling us how to meet the living Jesus. I would have to come back. While I waited for the next meeting, I thought deeply about what it could mean if Jesus really were alive. I didn't know how he would change my life, but I knew my life needed to change. Perhaps he was the one who saw the real me and would help me become all I longed to be.

When the date for the next meeting arrived a few days later, my friend and I returned. I even brought another friend along. After the meeting, I hurried to the stage, where the young man promised to introduce me to Jesus. I prayed a prayer, hoping God would hear and let me know these promises were true. And then I went home. As I lay in bed that night, I wondered if I would wake up the next morning feeling foolish for my presumption that God, who created the universe, could passionately love me, a troubled girl who had nothing to offer in return—nothing except my life, which didn't amount to much.

I awoke the next morning with an assurance of love I could neither explain nor deny. It was the assurance that God knew me, saw beyond the garbage, and loved me. Somehow I caught a glimpse of myself as seen through his eyes, and hope began to grow inside me once again. This vision God had of me was far different from what others saw when they looked at me. It was even different from what I saw when I looked at myself. But I began to believe in his power to transform me into the woman he had planned for me to become.

That day began a season of my life that was filled with miraculous moments shared, promises believed, prayers answered, rich friendships formed, and lives changed forever in wonderful ways. Throughout my high school years people were being touched and changed by what national magazines were calling "The Jesus Movement." It was a time of knowing his touch, feeling the sway of his Spirit, moving to the music of his love, and being dizzy-headed with hope for the future. I did not realize then the turns my life would still have to take to lift me out of the garbage around me.

GARBAGE COMES IN MANY different forms. You may feel as though you've been sitting among the garbage your entire life, that you have never learned to rise above the circumstances that keep people from knowing and loving the real you. Or you may know what it's like to rise above the garbage from your past, but occasional situations make you feel as though you're right back where you started. Your garbage may be being stuck doing a job that doesn't display your full potential, being trapped in an abusive relationship, or trying to escape a shameful past, or it may be as simple as being caught up in an everyday routine that is unfulfilling. As the days and years pass by, you feel like you've never started to live—at least not in a way that expresses the wonder you once believed was hidden inside you. If so, you are not alone. We all long for a place in life where we can be known and loved for who we are, where the garbage that surrounds us—even the garbage we create—doesn't obscure the beauty of the person inside.

While your life story is unique, there *are* longings of the heart that seem to be universal: the desire to find true love, the desire that someone will affirm our inherent value regardless of our situation, the hope that we can change. In this regard, we each need a Cinderella story of our own. God finds each of us in the cinders of a less than perfect world, held back from the life we dream of living. He longs to raise us up to a high position, transform us, and grant us his power, so he seeks us out, inviting each of us to dance with him.

Dancing in the arms of God is a relationship between you and God that is based on love and mutual respect. The two of you communicate in a close, intimate setting. He holds you, but his embrace is the embrace of a lover, not the restraint of an oppressor. As partners in this dance, God leads, and you let him, moving with the flow of his leading. You are not enveloped in God, losing your identity as a unique person; you are who you are, retaining your freedom and individuality at every turn.

Trying to create a mental picture of yourself dancing in the arms of God may prove difficult. After all, although God is real, you can't see him—at least not in this world. Think about what it would be like to have an invisible dance partner. Anyone looking on would see only you and the influence your partner had on you. If he lifted you up and twirled you around, those watching would be astounded because it would look as though you were doing these incredible feats on your own. Yet that is what a relationship with God is like. While you experience his power to move and lift you, others see only you. That's okay. As you continue dancing, others may never see God, but they won't be able to deny what he is doing in your life.

• • •

WHEN I FIRST BEGAN a relationship with God, I remember my bumbling attempts to explain what was happening in my life. I stumbled through a prayer on a Wednesday night, was handed a Bible, told to read it, pray daily, and come back for the next meeting on Saturday. I went to school the next day, excited to tell my friends something significant had happened to me. Although no one could see anything different, I now had an invisible partner!

At lunchtime I joined the circle of kids in the athletic field where we all smoked pot (far enough away from campus so that the teachers wouldn't catch us). My friends may have suspected something unusual when I passed the joint without smoking it. Then I made my grand announcement: "I got saved last night."

A boy named Roger asked, "Saved from what?"

That threw me for a moment. The jargon was still new to me. "I don't know yet," I said. "I suppose they will tell me on Saturday." Words alone were insufficient when I tried to introduce others to my invisible partner or describe the love that was growing, unexplained, in my heart.

When I went back on Saturday, I stayed after the concert for a meeting called Afterglow. I wanted to be closer to God, to feel his touch. I wanted to express the love I had for him. Like a girl awkwardly trying to express her heart with a first kiss, I closed my eyes as we sang a chorus about God being right there, moving among us.

As we sang the chorus over and over, again and again, I sensed God's presence. He *was* moving among us, a crowd of teenagers hungry for love, yet spiritually inexperienced. Everyone quieted themselves.

The man leading the meeting said, "Jesus is here this very moment. He can do the same miracles today that he did when he walked on earth. He will meet your deepest needs if you will only ask."

I had suffered recurrent ear infections from my earliest childhood, and just a few months previous to this meeting I had had an infection so severe it had ruptured my eardrum. Although my doctor warned me to keep water out of my ear, I disobeyed and jumped off the high dive at the school swimming pool, which resulted in a seventy percent hearing loss.

When the man leading Afterglow said Jesus was there among us, I wondered if God could touch my ears. It wasn't a request; it was just a thought. But at that moment I thought I heard rain softly falling on the canvas above me. The man on the stage said, "I think the Lord just healed someone's ears here on the left side of the room." He pointed in my direction. Me! It was me! I could hear him clearly!

The next day I asked the school nurse to administer a hearing test. She said she didn't see why I had to have one immediately, but she agreed. The test showed my hearing was perfect! I smiled broadly and told her it hadn't always been that way.

AT FIRST CINDERELLA JUST SAT in the corner among the ashes, dreaming of going to the ball and dancing in the arms of the prince. But what if the author had left Cinderella in the ashes, pointing out how happy she was with her dreams of grandeur instead of empowering her to make her dreams come true? Something inside us cries out against such an ending; it clashes with our expectations of "happily ever after." We don't want to see Cinderella dream of attending the ball unless she ends up actually going and dancing with the prince. We want her to overcome every obstacle in order for her to live out her dreams.

There is a real ball, a real palace, for each Cinderella. It's a spiritual realm where you can know God, where you are known and loved for who you are, where the garbage surrounding you doesn't obscure the beauty God sees in you. There God will free you from the bondage of your present condition and give you his power to change. He alone can see past the garbage to the girl, and beyond the girl to the woman you can become.

TWO

Someday My Prince Will Come

Expecting a man to fulfill you as a woman

CINDERELLA HOPED THAT SOMEDAY her prince would come to rescue her from her drudgery and bring her freedom and fulfillment. And her dreams came true!

Many girls today grow up hoping that someday a man (the right man) will come to complete them, give their lives meaning, and fulfill their deepest needs. Perhaps the desire for personal fulfillment is valid, but their hope is misplaced when they expect a man to supply the fulfillment they seek.

When I was a little girl, I remember how safe and loved I felt whenever I curled up in my stepfather Abie's lap on cold mornings. His love was characterized by indulgence: he made liver and onions disappear from my plate at dinnertime (to be replaced by peanut butter and jelly), took me on walks to the park, gave me goodies saved from his lunch, and let me stay up past my bedtime to hear him play guitar and sing with his friends. When I played dress-up, pretending to be a princess, he poured on me the adoration a princess deserves. He cherished me, and many of my early concepts of love were formed in the mold of his undemanding, adoring love.

I was six when we found out Abie had emphysema. I didn't understand that he was going to die. I curled up as close as I could to him on his hospital bed in our living room, longing to stay close to his love. When he moved to the hospital, I wrote letters and colored pictures for his wall because I was too young to visit. His death left a lonely place in my heart, a longing not only for him, but for any man who would love me as he had. Abie's love remained frozen in time, untested by the trials of my adolescence, perfect in my child's mind.

I soon turned my affections to my oldest brother, Richard. Richard was in prison when Abie died. I didn't know what he had done to be sent to prison, but it didn't matter. He was a hero to me, not because of any particular heroic feats, but because he loved me. He would run to greet me during our weekly visits, scoop me up in his big arms, and twirl me around until I couldn't stand from dizziness.

The happiest day of my childhood was the day Richard was released from prison. Finally, I could see him or talk with him on the phone whenever I wanted! Soon Richard found a good job, married, and began a family. He was often at our house, playing his guitar and singing country songs. I would sit on his knee with his guitar wrapped around me while he strummed and sang. Then he would place my fingers on the strings and try to teach me to play. The strumming of those guitar strings reverberated with more than music; they echoed with memories of Abie's guitar-playing, Abie's love.

When I was eleven, Richard was hit by a drunk driver while riding a motorcycle. He lived twenty-one days before dying two days before Christmas 1969. The day he died, his wife, Pat, gave birth to their second son. I was devastated, partially by the seeming injustice of life and partially because I had lost more than just my brother. I had once again lost someone who had loved me without condition and accepted me without reservation. My grief turned to rage: How could God let something like this happen? Why the father of young children? Why my brother? How could God take away another person who loved me?

Until Richard's death, I accepted God as I accepted everything around me. I had gone to Sunday school and knew the Bible, but I had never before found it necessary to question God. Now I was in heated revolt. I demanded an explanation. Wasn't God supposed to be love personified? If he was, how could he let this happen? How could he allow me to be robbed of one who loved me so? That night, after the funeral, I was more distraught and angry than sad. I went into my bedroom alone and got down on my knees beside my bed. "God," I prayed, "I don't know how you could let this happen. I have to know, otherwise how can I ever trust you? You have to explain it to me. If you don't, I will never speak to you again!"

Tearfully, I fell into an exhausted sleep. Then, in a dream (I don't know what else to call it), I found myself being shaken from sleep by Richard. He was wearing his favorite clothes—Levi's 501 jeans and a white T-shirt. His hair flowed in its natural brown waves, not slicked back as it had been for the funeral. His smile was radiant. He took me on his knee and held me close while I cried and laughed and tried to take it all in, tried to figure out if his death and funeral were just a bad dream.

Richard said, "Connie, I know you're upset and you don't understand. Someday you will. I promise. I'm with God now, and I'm happier than I ever dreamed I could be. You need to tell Mom and Pat that I am safe with God. God heard your prayers. He's going to use you to bring our whole family to know him."

I didn't speak. It was as though a new reality surrounded me. Then he said, "I have to go back now. Don't worry about me. Just tell the others what I said." Then he tucked me back into bed, kissed my forehead, and sleep came over me.

When I awoke, this dream seemed quite strange to me. I didn't know what to make of it and didn't tell anyone about it for some time. When I did ask my older sisters if Richard was at peace with God before he died, they said he seemed to know somehow that he was going to die soon. Just prior to the accident Richard had expressed faith in Christ and a desire to become part of a church. He had also purchased life insurance just weeks before he died. It was comforting to think that perhaps God was looking out for his small children. Richard's prediction that I would lead the rest of our family to God didn't make sense to me until I became a Christian, but it also proved true. Little did I know then that I would be the first one in our family to share my faith openly, and that God would use my witness to influence other members of our family who came to faith after me.

Despite the assurance I gained from my dream that Richard was with God, it didn't help satisfy my growing hunger for someone to fill the deficit of love in my life. In fact, one of the reasons I responded enthusiastically when I was introduced to Jesus and his love for me was partially because Jesus had already died and would never die again. I yearned for love from someone I knew would not die and leave me.

As I MADE MY WAY through adolescence I began to hunger for another kind of relationship. Much of my seventeenth summer was spent with my best friend, Jonnine, dating a bit and reflecting for hours on end over our hopes for romance. We stayed up late, shared our joys and sorrows, and chronicled our growing experience with the opposite sex in stories and poems.

I find it more than mere coincidence that the particular young man I set my sights on played guitar magnificently—there was still something of the little girl within me longing for a man to surround me with his music. The image I had of him may or may not have had anything to do with the person he was; I know it had everything to do with the hunger I felt because of the love I lost while growing up. I wanted this boy to be my prince, my ideal man who would love me and fill the void I held inside.

While we maintained an intense and often turbulent friendship throughout high school, I was disappointed in my hopes for romance. When I moved away to college, he promised to write. My disappointment grew each day a letter from him did not arrive.

One day as I turned away from my empty mailbox and headed back toward my dorm, I sensed God trying to get through to me. I stopped on a bridge at the center of campus and prayed silently, still weighed down with disappointment. "What is it, Lord? What are you trying to tell me?" I asked.

I looked out past the stained glass of the chapel toward the sea. Clouds covered the skies, painting the ocean with shades of gray. Then I spotted a break in the clouds where brilliant sunlight was breaking through, spilling a circle of light on the darkened surface of the waters. I heard no voice, but the thought came to my mind that I should read Psalm 45. I don't recall if I had read this psalm previously; if I had, I didn't remember what it was about.

I hurried to my dorm, curious about what the passage might say. I half expected that I was playing games with myself, but there was the outside chance that the psalm might say something applicable to my situation. What I read that day changed my life forever:

Listen, O daughter, consider and give ear:
Forget your people and your father's house.
The king is enthralled by your beauty;
honor him, for he is your lord. . . .
All glorious is the princess within her chamber;
her gown is interwoven with gold.
In embroidered garments she is led to the king;
her virgin companions follow her and are brought to you.
They are led in with joy and gladness;
they enter the palace of the king.

(Psalm 45:10–11, 13–15)

God was letting me know that he was my prince, my king. The people I grew up with, the boy I looked to in hopes that he would be my prince—none of these relationships could satisfy my deepest needs. Only God could lead me to true fulfillment, and he was enthralled with my beauty.

Even though God showed me the truth that day, I didn't apply it immediately. I was still prone to bouts of self-pity, and that summer I filled my journal while trying to make peace with the rejection I felt from this young man.

IT ISN'T IN VOGUE for a nineties woman to admit she grew up hoping "someday my prince will come," yet many girls and women still do secretly hold on to that very wish. The fact is, any woman who thinks a mortal man will fulfill her as a woman will eventually be disappointed.

A woman who insists on placing all her needs and demands for social interaction, intellectual stimulation, practical help, and love on one man may find him recoiling, feeling smothered and consumed. A man who is expected to play God in terms of fulfill-

ing a woman's needs might play God by trying to control her or
shape her into who *he* wants her to be instead of who God created
her to be. And the woman in such a relationship may find herself
giving up some of her power and dignity in exchange for having a
man take over responsibility for her life.

It is not unreasonable to expect your father to protect, nurture, provide for, and help you grow as a child. Nor is it unreasonable to expect a husband to fulfill his marriage commitment to
remain faithful to you, love you, and maintain honesty and respect
within your relationship. But expecting a man to fulfill you and
meet your deepest needs puts that man in a place only God should
hold in your life. While God created a man and a woman to com-
pliment each other in a satisfying way, no human being was
intended to completely meet the deepest needs of another. If a
man could fulfill your life, why would you hunger for and seek
God? Why would you venture to discover your own potential,
power, talents, and abilities?

Many women who have been hurt and disappointed in relationships with men have reacted against all men. They have turned
to self-reliance or to other women to fill the void and heal the
hurts they have suffered. But looking only to yourself or other
women to give you fulfillment is as faulty as expecting a man to
fulfill you. It is not gender that makes men unable to fulfill your
deepest needs; it is human frailty.

Our desires for fulfillment, acceptance, unconditional love,
security, and validation are good. We need only transfer these
desires to the One capable of fulfilling them. Throughout the
Bible God reveals himself as father, husband, and brother. He
offers to actively compensate for the failures of men in your life.
When you need to depend on someone, call out to God. Whisper
a prayer. Write him a note. Ask him to reveal himself to you in a

way you can comprehend. Ask for wisdom with which to understand situations beyond your comprehension. Even if you feel distant from God, perhaps wondering why he allows you to remain in a difficult situation, that's okay. You can still look to him. He is your prince.

God promises that the heart that seeks him sincerely will find him. He wants to prove to you that this promise is true. Let him. Whenever you sense a hunger in your soul, a desire left unquenched, a disappointment that defeats you, turn to him and ask him to fill your deepest needs in the appropriate way. Then look for your life to change.

I do not advocate putting your reliance on God in such a way that you exempt a man from fulfilling his roles and commitments. Many women who are overly dependent on men fear displeasing them to the extent that they overlook the man's negligence and irresponsible behavior. These women may be more inclined to plead, whine, and placate their husbands, or to try to manipulate them into loving them. By developing a relationship with God and putting him first in your life, you gain the confidence to hold a man accountable to fulfill *his* roles.

MY FATHER LOVED ME with all his heart. He was, however, a compulsive gambler. Throughout my childhood and adolescence, he made promise after promise of what he was going to do for me if he hit the jackpot or if his horse won the race. I know these promises came from a sincere desire to make me happy, but when I believed them, I was often disappointed.

Once, when I was in fourth grade, he had to flee to Alaska to escape loan sharks. When I was in high school, his losses outnumbered his wins to the extent that he was financially bankrupt. As time for college approached, I feared I wouldn't be able to attend a good school because we had no money. And just as I was about to graduate, we lost our home.

Most kids move away from their parents. My dad and stepmother were going to have to move away from me. They planned to go back to Arkansas where they had relatives. At that moment I needed God to provide for me those things my father should have provided, but couldn't.

My grades and test scores were good, so I had no trouble qualifying for college. I consoled myself by thinking at least I could attend somewhere, although it probably wouldn't be highly-rated. I began to work with a counselor named Patricia, applying to schools with the lowest tuition. In May of 1976 I prepared to go to a small school that didn't excite me very much.

Then something happened one day as I was praying. I had taken some time to be quiet before God. While calmly listening, a thought came to me, as though God were speaking directly to me: *Connie, have you read in my word where I say, "Delight yourself in me and I will give you the desires of your heart"?*

I was familiar with that promise. Sure.

Well, if you were to list the true desires of your heart regarding college, what would you list?

I wrote a list: (1) I wanted a school with an excellent reputation for academics with a Christian emphasis, but not a Bible college. (2) I wanted the school to be within driving distance of my church. (3) I wanted to be able to live on campus. (4) I needed money for full tuition, books, living expenses, and room and board. (5) If this was really God talking (and not just my mind playing tricks on me), he would have to direct me to the school. (6) I would need to be accepted for the upcoming year (the deadlines for registration were already past). (7) I would have to finalize all the plans within two weeks, because my commitment to the other school would be sealed at that time.

I didn't quite know what to make of this exchange. I figured that if it wasn't God speaking, no one would ever have to know. If it was, hey, how could I let this kind of opportunity pass me by? The next day as I was walking by the counseling office, Patricia motioned me inside.

"I'm so glad you came by. I was thinking maybe we should have you apply to Pepperdine University."

I wasn't very familiar with the school; I had heard only that it was expensive and private. "Pepperdine?" I frowned. "Can you tell me a little about it?"

"Well, it's not a Bible school. It has an excellent reputation for academics as a private liberal arts college, and it does have a Christian emphasis."

That was enough to get my attention. "Where is it located?"

She showed me Malibu on a map. It was closer to my church than where I was currently living. She went on to describe the beautiful campus overlooking the ocean, and she mentioned that they strongly urged freshmen to live on campus in the new dorms. We filled out the application. Within one week I received a letter of acceptance and enough scholarship and grant money to cover full tuition, room and board, books, and living expenses. God had taken care of me. As my heavenly Father, he did for me what my earthly father dreamed of doing, wished he could do, but failed to do because of his human frailty.

When I graduated from Pepperdine four years later, Dad was so proud. My reliance on my heavenly Father had not displaced him. It only took up the slack, answering Dad's prayers as well as my own.

When you accept that no mere mortal will fulfill you, you too can be freed from disappointment to begin a new way of life. By transferring your ultimate dependence to God, you will gain assurance of his unfailing love, power to set boundaries, and power to hold others accountable. With God as your prince, you will be able to face difficulties with confidence that no matter who dies or fails you, you can still be a fulfilled person and fulfill the dreams God has in store for you.

THREE

Life Among the Ashes

*Dealing with disillusionment and the
destruction of your dreams*

H<small>ER NAME WAS</small> E<small>LLA</small>, but most
people forgot that. The cinders in which she sat so darkened her
existence that almost everyone came to identify her with her misfortune. She became known as Cinder-ella. All those who were
supposed to take care of Cinderella had either abandoned her
through death or abused her for their own purposes. Her own
childhood dreams of what life would be had turned to disillusionment with the death of her father. Cinderella had to decide how to
face her future while sitting among the cinders.

We all have to deal with what I call the cinders of life: circumstances that are not what we dreamed of as a child. Just as
Cinderella was abused and soiled, experiences beyond our control
can darken our lives, leaving us fearful, bitter, brokenhearted, and
beaten down. Living too long among the cinders will mar our true
identities and keep us from becoming the women God created us
to be. Regardless of what happens to us, we don't have to live

forever among the cinders of what might have been. We must choose whether to make the cinders part of our identity or part of our past.

RECENTLY, FIRE STORMS CAME raging through the tender dry brush of the Southern California hills. Without respect for the homes, hopes, and dreams of the people who lived there, the fires raged through the affluent seaside community of Laguna Beach. After the fires had been contained and evacuation orders lifted, residents headed back to see what was left of their homes.

I saw a woman on the evening news sifting through the debris. Her clothes were covered with sooty black ash, her tired face etched in an expression of stunned disbelief. Her grown daughter raced over to show her a teacup salvaged from the ruins of the once-fine home.

"It's all gone," the woman mumbled within earshot of the reporter's microphone. "Everything I've worked for . . . everything we have . . . gone. There's nothing left. Nothing. A teacup. That's all that's left of our lives." The woman was in the throes of shock, the initial realization that the fires had reduced her home, her mementos of family life, and her treasured belongings to a pile of cinders.

A couple of months later, a friend of mine received a Christmas card from a friend who also lived in Laguna Beach. The picture on the front showed the charred remains of a home. All that was left standing was the fireplace—everything else was reduced to ashes. The members of the family sat smiling in front of the fireplace in their Christmas outfits, their Christmas stockings hanging above them on the blackened brick.

The greeting on the card read "From Our House To Yours, Merry Christmas!" The message inside was laced with faith and good humor. The woman explained, "I usually include a letter chronicling the events of the previous year, but unfortunately my calendar burned in the fire. I think it was a good year, though; we're all still here and in good health. We're living in a hotel until the insurance comes through, so it feels like we are on some kind of bizarre vacation. But we're sure we'll be back in our home by next year, so don't throw away our address." Even though the fire had left this woman and her family sitting amidst the cinders, it couldn't consume their hope for the future!

When I talk about the fires of life, I speak figuratively of anything that may occur to destroy your life and your dreams of what life was supposed to be. Just as these two women had no control over the fires that destroyed their homes, we have no control over many of life's difficulties that can bring destruction, leaving us with only charred remains of what we once dreamed of, worked to build, and cherished. Yet where one woman was devastated, the other was able to face the future with hope and optimism.

Every woman will face times of suffering and loss, and while we can't always control what happens to us, we *can* choose how to deal with the fires of destruction and the charred remains of our dreams. It is this choice that determines the ultimate effect those events will have on our lives.

THE CINDERELLA STORY is told differently from one culture to another. In the English versions, the heroine's name is Cinderella, associated with the cinders. In these versions, Cinderella is forced to live among the cinders by her wicked stepmother. In the German tale by the Brothers Grimm, the heroine's name is

Aschenputtel. *Aschenputtel* means "a person who stirs around in the ashes." In the German version, as well as Charles Perrault's French tale, Aschenputtel is not forced to live among the cinders but rather, she chooses to sleep among the ashes near the fireplace to keep warm. Ashes carry with them connotations of purity and deep mourning, whereas cinders refer to blackness and dirtiness. These two different ways of telling the story—being forced to live in the cinders versus choosing to live among the ashes—represent two starkly different ways a woman can choose to deal with the fires of life.

Cinders are the charred remains of what was burned. Where there are cinders there is still fuel for the fire. Living amidst the cinders is characterized by

- holding on to the remains of the past
- smoldering in bitterness and resentment
- trying to rebuild what was lost instead of building something new
- insisting on making someone pay for something that happened
- being stuck, unable to get on with life after the destruction
- being mired in self-pity
- taking on an identity associated with the misfortune that has occurred

While in college, I met a young woman who I will call Mara. On Mara's honeymoon, she and her husband were in a serious car accident. Mara was paralyzed and would need to use a wheelchair for the rest of her life. Her husband, who had vowed to love her and keep her, for better or for worse, in sickness and in health, dissolved the marriage and left without saying good-bye. Everything

Mara dreamed of was destroyed. She came home to live with her parents.

I met Mara before my junior year, while I was looking for a place to live off campus. Her parents sought a companion and helper for her in exchange for room and board. I accepted the position, but after one week I knew the situation was too much for me. Mara exuded anger and bitterness. If I was late getting back from class, Mara attacked with a vengeance. In her eyes, her life was over. She had little interest in developing a new life; she was stuck in the ruins of the life that was destroyed and stolen from her by misfortune. She would not abide any mention of God, since she held him ultimately to blame. I apologized to Mara and her family and resigned from the position.

Mara was living among the cinders—the charred remains of her life and destroyed dreams. The first fire destroyed her dreams and physical mobility. And now the fire that smoldered among the cinders was destroying her spirit, her hope for the future, and her joy.

Beware of drawing your identity from what you have suffered. We are all familiar with the caricatured image of the martyr, the woman who makes a production out of enduring suffering by recounting episodes of how life has done her wrong and recalling details from decades of accumulated pain. Some women who have been victimized fall into the trap of seeing themselves as victims for so long that they set themselves up to be further victimized.

When God looks at you, he doesn't see a woman permanently marred by the cinders of life. Instead, he sees the woman he created you to become, the woman he loves. He sees someone whose inner beauty may be temporarily obscured by current painful circumstances. God doesn't want you to live permanently among the charred remains of your dreams. He wants you to have a relationship with him that changes the way you see yourself, the way you perceive your life, and how you deal with life's difficulties.

Ashes are different from cinders. They are the remains of a fire that has completely consumed what was burned. With ashes there is nothing more to burn. There can be no more destruction because there is nothing left to lose. Living among the ashes is characterized by

- surrender of all to God in the midst of painful circumstances
- finishing the process of working through painful emotions
- letting go of the past and facing a new reality with honest acceptance
- weeding out bitterness and resentment as they surface
- looking to build something new instead of trying to recreate the past
- relinquishing demands that someone must pay for what happened
- taking small steps to get on with life
- refusing to live in self-pity

Joni Eareckson Tada is a glowing example of life among the ashes. As a teenager Joni broke her neck in a diving accident. She was left a paraplegic. Her book *Joni* tells the story of how she sifted through the cinders of her life and dreams until she finally surrendered what was left of her life to God. She still had to work through painful physical recovery and anguished emotions as she grieved her losses, but she determined to let go of the past and see what God would have for her in the future. She chose not to ignore or tolerate resentment, bitterness, or self-pity. Instead, she faced these and sought God's help to keep them from taking root in her spirit. Joni has gone on to become an accomplished singer, artist (drawing and painting with her mouth), speaker, author, and advocate for those with handicaps of all kinds.

Joni chose to make the cinders of her life a burnt offering to God. Once she let go of the past and her destroyed dreams, God began to build her future. Her life now brings hope to those who hear her story. The fires of life may have destroyed Joni's dreams and physical mobility, but once she made the rest of her life a sacrifice to God, there was nothing left to become fuel for the inner fires that could have destroyed her spirit, her hope for the future, and her joy.

I WAS A YOUNG woman the last time I had to choose whether or not I would surrender my life to God. At that point, I cherished hopes for a happy life. I wanted to make a difference in the world. I wanted a loving husband, a healthy family, and a career of some significance. In eighth grade I had decided the best career in the world would be to write books. But when I became a Christian, I changed my aspirations: I wanted to reach young people with God's love.

I married Patrick the summer before my senior year of college. For the next ten years I pursued my dreams for career, marriage, and family life. I worked hard to become the best youth worker I could become, successfully developing youth ministries in several churches. Our marriage was great. I enjoyed being a mother to my little girl and looked forward to having other children. And then my husband and I accepted a position working together in youth ministry at a large church, an event which brought together all the elements of life I had hoped for.

My faithfulness and hard work seemed to be paying off until the day my husband confessed that he had been unfaithful to me. It would have been easier to believe the moon had fallen from the sky. This was impossible. I had the perfect husband. He loved the Lord. He loved his family. He loved the kids in our youth group. He was so much more than I had hoped for in a husband—but I was to find out he was also much more than I had known.

Although at first my mind refused to believe him, the details I tearfully demanded and he haltingly supplied tore away my illusions. As reality forced its way into my mind, I was terribly shaken. Everything I once trusted became suspect. I wondered how I could have lived with him and his secrets all these years and never suspected anything. Thankfully, Pat committed himself to being honest with me, himself, and God. He eagerly sought professional help to work through the issues underlying his infidelity. He renewed his commitment to our marriage and broke off all inappropriate behavior. Because of this, I hoped we could solve our problems with God's help and keep our marriage together. One week after he confessed to me, I found out I was pregnant.

One concern overwhelmed all others when I considered the implications of our situation: *What would this do to our kids in the youth ministry?* The thought of how this betrayal might impact their lives terrified me. I became consumed with the desire to protect them and help them see God work in this terrible situation.

I wanted to talk to our pastor, until Pat told me that, although the pastor did not know of his continuing problem, he *had* known of Pat's previous infidelity before we came on staff with his church. The pastor had agreed with Pat to keep his secret from me. This obliterated my trust in the pastor as well. I felt twice betrayed.

Decisions had to be made, and I was in no condition to think clearly. I had to reexamine my entire marriage, family life, ministry, and understanding of God—after all, he had allowed this to happen without giving me a clue. The next few weeks and months were turbulent, filled with rage and pain beyond any I had known.

We talked with five Christian counselors. All five agreed Pat and I should take time to stabilize our marriage before deciding if and when to tell our pastor. We remained in counseling five months, traveling to another town to protect our privacy. The combination of being honest with me, receiving Christian counseling, and the hope of a new child helped Pat manage his temptations. Spiritually he seemed back on track, accepting God's forgiveness and mine.

During those five months we finalized our calendar for the coming year of ministry. I worked hard to make sure the kids in our youth group would be well cared for regardless of what happened to Pat. In January 1989 we heard Stephen Arterburn speak about issues related to our situation. He warned that whenever sin recurs, deeper issues must be resolved. We confided our situation to Stephen, who recommended inpatient care and counseling for Pat at New Life Treatment Center. We determined to get whatever help was necessary to resolve the underlying issues.

It was then that we decided to tell our pastor. He immediately terminated Pat's position. When the question was raised regarding whether my position would be terminated as well, the pastor replied emphatically, "Of course not, Connie hasn't sinned! There are no grounds for termination." From nine in the morning until ten that night we underwent questioning before the pastoral staff and an emergency meeting of the board.

The ordeal of going over every shame-filled detail with so many people was incredibly devastating. Pat desperately needed reassurance in the grace of God. (After all, he had repented eight months earlier, confessed to me, remained in counseling, and had not fallen back into sin.) Still, those hearing of his infidelity reacted as though he was still in sin. The newness of the revelation overshadowed all we had done to overcome the sin and its effects.

The next day I had five hundred junior high kids arriving for an event I had been planning for months. I arrived at church with Pat. He was dangerously unstable. I feared he might attempt suicide, so I asked if one of the staff members would stay with him.

"If you care so much about him, you go home with him," the administrative pastor responded without emotion. "We can handle things here without you." One of the volunteers offered to go with him. The administrative pastor closed his door—and, we assumed, his heart—to us.

The event was a great success, but that didn't seem to matter to those in power. Later that night the senior pastor informed us they would make a public announcement to the congregation the following day during both services. Pat could choose to make his own confession or to have the pastor do it. Pat chose to make his own statement for the sake of the kids. He had to write it out so that it could be approved. I too prepared a statement reflecting our certain hope that the Lord could redeem this situation.

When the pastor previewed Pat's statement, he made him remove his comment assuring the kids I would still be there to help them through this. I panicked. When they refused my request to make any statement or speak to the kids before, during, or after the service, my panic escalated into near hysteria. I begged, reasoned, pleaded, demanded. I lost all sense of decorum. I finally convinced them of the danger of making this announcement without giving the kids some opportunity to process their shock and grief. The pastor conceded. We could wait in a secluded room after each service and receive any kids or parents who wanted to talk with us.

I can't adequately describe the heart-wrenching emotions I felt while standing on the platform where we had been the recipients of so much love and approval, and looking into the eyes of our kids, their parents, and our volunteers as they received this unbelievable news. You will have to imagine it for yourself. Just touching the edges of my memories of that day makes me come apart all over again.

After the service, the kids, their parents, and our friends brought us their love and grief, fear and sorrow. Many affirmed their continuing love, and some confessed personal struggles with sexual issues.

One girl in particular stands out in my memory. If our group had been a litter of puppies, she would have been the beloved runt of the litter. She came to us with slight physical disabilities and awkward social skills. She was hungry for God and a place to belong. In our ministry she had found her place and blossomed. Now she feared someone would take us away from her.

"They aren't going to take you away from us, are they?" she kept asking me. "Are they?"

I looked around for someone to answer that question, but all eyes were averted. She collapsed on the floor, curled up in a fetal position, clutched my leg, and sobbed uncontrollably as she choked out her pleas. "Don't leave us! Please, tell them how much we need you. Don't let them take you away." Her mother pried her from me and led her off.

Within a few days the board terminated both our salaries with two weeks' pay. Our insurance would be terminated as soon as Pat completed treatment at New Life. As a result, we could no longer afford professional counseling. The board also immediately terminated our daughter's preschool tuition allowance at the church-run school.

The following days were awash in a sea of tears and unfathomable grief. Relatives took our daughter, Casey (who was four at the time), because we were unable to care for her. Our friend, Rayna, took us into her home. I needed to talk to figure out what was happening. Night and day, I talked about the kids in the youth group, about what needed to happen to keep the ministry going. Our best volunteers took turns, listening for hours on end, consoling me as I fought off the realization that my kids were being taken away. When exhaustion compelled me to sleep, I had nightmares. Kids from the youth group were crying and reaching out for me. I ran to them but fences and barbed wire stopped me, keeping us apart.

After a week we tried to go home, but found we were no longer sufficient protection for each other. Now I too was suicidal. Youth ministry was my passion, my identity. If that was taken away, who was I? How could I go on? Our love for Casey and the child I carried drove us back to the safety of Rayna and Larry's house.

No one addressed the issue of what my position would be in light of Pat's termination. I clung to the pastor's promise that my position would not be terminated. The senior pastor and administrative pastor conducted our monthly meeting of volunteers, using the opportunity to try to weave a scriptural explanation as to why I should be removed from ministry. They inferred that there was more to the story about me than people knew and suggested that since Pat and I were "one flesh" in marriage, his fall invalidated my ministry.

Pat became dangerously unstable, forcing us to seek immediate care for him at New Life Treatment Center. No one in church leadership spoke to me during the two weeks Pat was away. I was home alone, five months pregnant, and brokenhearted. When I finally did receive a call from the church, I was sure it would be someone calling to comfort me or talk about the plan for resuming the ministry under my leadership. Instead, our former secretary notified me that I must vacate our office—immediately. This was more than I could bear. I feared I'd lose the baby if I were forced to take down pictures of our youth group from the wall and pack everything away. I begged them to wait for Pat to come home. Why should I be forced to bear this burden alone? I asked to talk to the administrative pastor, who had given the order. He wouldn't come to the phone. He sent the secretary back with a message: "Either vacate your office today, or we'll pack your things and leave them on the curb."

I called Rayna to help me. Somehow we vacated the office. The final insult came when the secretary sheepishly told us she was required to watch us and make copies of any papers removed from the office, as though I would steal something. Within one day, our former office was freshly painted (I think *whitewashed* describes it better).

By the time Pat got out of the hospital two weeks later, I felt *I* needed to go in. The sense of betrayal and devastation wrought in my life by how the church leadership had treated me far exceeded Pat's betrayal. After we came home from the hospital, we and the kids in the youth group awaited the board's decree on the fate of our ministry and any possibility of restoration. The board banned Pat from ministry for two years. If he submitted to the church's (non-existent) restoration plan, he could be considered for possible ministry in the future.

There was no mention of restoration for me. According to the board, I needed no restoration because I hadn't sinned and had not been fired. They said nothing on the record regarding my ministry—they simply cut off my salary and benefits and would not let me attend youth ministry functions. I requested a hearing before the board (Even Sapphira received an individual trial before her execution!), but any time I tried to bring up my reinstatement, I was greeted with either anger or tense silence. It was painfully obvious that I was seen as merely an extension of my husband.

The church leaders even refused to let me address the board to discuss how they could implement the youth ministry calendar and help the kids through their grief and confusion. Instead they had one Bible study on dealing with pain, followed by a pizza party. They promised the kids an opportunity to speak with us "when we were feeling better," leading them to believe we chose not to talk with them. After that they never mentioned us again, nor did they keep their promise to let the kids talk with us. Amy, one of our high school girls, remarked, "I thought love was supposed to cover a multitude of sins, not one sin wipe out a multitude of love." All the anger, sadness, fear, disillusionment, despair, and other emotions the kids were feeling were supposed to be swept under the rug. No one on staff wanted to talk about it.

Since there was no plan for restoration, we wrote one under our counselor's direction. The board approved it. We set up a men's support group for Pat, kept in touch with our therapist by telephone, and hoped for the day we could minister again. Being five months pregnant made finding new employment unfeasible, so I spent my days and nights living among the cinders, refusing to let go. I became obsessed with proving their mistake. I did everything in my power to get my position back, clinging to the identity I found in my work. I fumed, argued, reasoned; I pleaded for mercy; I demanded justice. I deluded myself into believing they were going to see the error of their ways and give me back my position. My prayers to God centered on the hope that he would miraculously pick up the charred cinders that remained of my life and rebuild it as it had been before. During that season I did not pray, "Father, your will be done." I wanted *my* will to be done. At my insistence, we stayed at that church for an entire year as I waited for God to answer my prayers the way I wanted them answered.

Over the course of time the reality of the situation took its toll. The church hired a new youth pastor. I was unable to work because I had a new baby. The depressed economy made it extremely difficult for Pat to find work. He found employment after several weeks, but nothing near enough to make up for the loss of both our salaries. Friends helped us immensely, but it grew more apparent day by day that if we didn't make some kind of move toward a better future, we would lose our home. I was faced with a moment of decision: Would I surrender to the reality of our situation and let go of my demands that everything work out the way I thought it was "supposed" to, or would I stay among the cinders, continuing to protest what had happened to me?

Pat and I prayed: "Lord, if you want us to go in a different direction, please lead us. We are falling apart. We don't want to lose our home. We need counseling we can't afford. Please show us what to do. If you show us, we will follow your lead."

This was a scary prayer for me. I had a lot of unfinished emotional business that I would have to face if we closed this chapter of our lives. I would have to relinquish everything to God—all my scenarios, all my demands, all my rights that had been violated, all the counts of injustice I held against those I believed had wronged me.

The process of laying my life down as a sacrifice to God was marked by tremendous struggle and inner turmoil. Until I made the decision to surrender, to relinquish my way, to let go of that which I desperately clung to, I felt as if I was in the throes of death rather than on the brink of a new life.

I remember talking this over with Rayna, who was there for me during my turmoil. She tells me now that she could see a dramatic change starting when I chose to surrender. The moment I let go, God took up our cause. It was as if God had waited for that very moment to release the power of heaven to change the course of our lives.

Pat called his therapist at New Life to ask for guidance now that I had become willing to consider a future other than the only one I had been willing to envision before. His therapist offered to give us free counseling if we moved back to southern California. Pat went to a career expo to seek employment down south and was offered a management position with a company located three miles from the counselor's office. We moved away from the charred remains of all the hopes I had grasped at for so long.

Less than a year after we moved, I was offered a job helping Jim Burns with the National Institute of Youth Ministry. While at the National Youth Ministry Convention, I happened to mention to Stephen Arterburn that I had aspirations to write. From that conversation came the opportunity to write the devotionals for *The Life Recovery Bible*. As I worked at identifying recovery principles found throughout the Bible, God worked on my heart. This was a season of grieving my losses, yet also growing to understand that God never wastes our pain and sorrows: He redeems them. After I successfully finished that project, numerous other writing projects sprang up, completely unsolicited.

I had not found it an easy thing to lay the cinders of my life before God and willingly allow him to consume them. I behaved more like the woman in the Laguna Beach fires sifting through the ruins while mumbling about how her life was over than the one who sent the humorous Christmas card. However, once I relinquished those cherished cinders, the remains of the life and dreams I had held dear, I was able to experience the power of Christ's resurrection. Life came only after death.

When all seemed lost amid these fiery trials, the most amazing thing happened. I found a hope in God that was independent of my hopes that he would do a particular thing. I realized that my hope was secure even though life was not. Like Cinderella in the ashes, I had to live through those troubles, work through the pressing conflicts with others, grieve my lost dreams, and grow, slowly and painfully, into a more mature woman. But the sense of security I found in God's arms once I considered everything a loss was incredible. In giving up everything, there was nothing left to come between us.

THERE IS GREAT POWER in choosing to surrender your life completely to God in the midst of suffering. Once you consider everything a total loss, you have nothing left to lose! There is great freedom in living among the ashes that is unknown to those who live among the cinders.

Here is what you need to do to move from life among the cinders to life among the ashes:

Recognize that God is always with you in the fiery difficulties of life. When the Hebrew people were taken captive by the Babylonians in 605 B.C., a group of devout young men were taken into training for service to the king of Babylon. A crisis arose when the king commanded all his subjects to worship a statue of the king's image. Being devout Jews, the young men refused. The king threatened to throw them into a furnace used to burn alive all who displeased the king. The young men said to the king, "If we are thrown into the blazing furnace, the God we serve is able to save us from it, and he will rescue us from your hand, O king. But even if he does not, we want you to know, O king, that we will not serve your gods or worship the image of gold you have set up" (Daniel 3:17–18).

This little speech did nothing more than infuriate the king, who then ordered the heat turned up seven times as hot as usual. The soldiers bound the men hand and foot and threw them into the flames. The king looked into the fire and was astounded by what he saw. He said to his officials, "Weren't there three men that we tied up and threw into the fire? . . . Look! I see four men walking around in the fire, unbound and unharmed, and the fourth looks like a son of the gods" (Daniel 3:24–25).

These young men literally offered their lives as a living sacrifice, a burnt offering to God. When they did, the fire did not destroy them. It destroyed only one thing: the ropes that bound them. And God was with them in the midst of the fire. Everyone could see it. Whenever we willingly accept the fires of life and look for God to be with us, suffering loses its power to destroy; rather, the fire acts as an agent to free us from those things that once bound us.

The king fearfully called them out of the fire, and he appointed them to positions of power and honor within his administration. God does not leave you alone when you go through the fires of life. He is with you in the fires and will bring you out to a new and better life. Believing this will give you the courage to face the fires of life courageously, with hope for the future.

Choose to surrender the cinders to God. Are you able to recreate your life by yourself? Or will you trust God to work his will out through the circumstances, even though things may turn out to be radically different? It will take time to recover emotionally from whatever pain you go through, but when you do find the strength to look toward the future, take whatever is left and surrender it to God. Then he can lead you toward a fulfilling life.

Invite God to do whatever he wants with your life. When you stop insisting life go the way you determine it must go, you open yourself up to possibilities you may have never dreamed of before. The choice I made to put aside my plans and invite God to do whatever he wanted with my life proved to be the beginning of a writing career I had hoped for long ago. Now, seven years after the crisis, my marriage is strong and satisfying, and I have a happy, healthy family. I am both humbled and awed to see how God used these twists in the plot to multiply the impact of my ministry.

Work toward forgiveness. Whenever there is a fire, people want to discover what caused it and who was responsible. I did the same thing. Much of my obsession revolved around tracing clues to find out who was responsible for what had been done to me. This is an important part of the healing process. In hurtful situations, including abuse of all kinds, you can't break free from the past unless you are willing to discover the truth about what happened to you and who is responsible.

There is a danger, however, of getting stuck at this point. Once you identify who is responsible, it is right and good to hold those who hurt you accountable for their actions. However, we don't live in a perfect world where those who cause the damage can be made to pay for it or repair it. After doing all you reasonably can to find justice, even if justice escapes you (as it often does in an imperfect world), you must let go of your demand that someone must pay for your pain and suffering.

To forgive does not mean you should act as though no one is to blame. Someone very well may be. But when you forgive, you transfer to God all remaining moral debts you are holding against those who have hurt you. These moral debts are part of the cinders you must choose to place on the altar and they make up part of your total sacrifice.

It is comforting for me to know that God sees our grievances as valid and does not discard them as unimportant. He promises to repay those who have hurt us, in his own way. I have seen God deal with those whose accounts I turned over to him.

Grieve your losses fully to find purity of spirit. Ashes are associated with both mourning and purity. Traditionally, those in mourning would cover themselves with ashes as a sign of intense sorrow. In the purification of gold, a fire is used to melt the gold so that impurities will rise to the top, where they can be skimmed off. After each firing, a time of cooling is allowed. Then the gold is melted again to bring up any remaining impurities. This same kind of purification process takes place as we suffer and grieve our losses.

I entered counseling to deal with the crisis in our marriage and in my career. But those were just surface issues. As I let myself grieve my losses, deeper losses and leftover pain from the past resurfaced. God could then heal the deep hurts that I hadn't been able to see before he allowed the fires of suffering to bring them to my attention. I now see how God was at work making good use of these fires (even though he did not cause them) in order to purify my heart.

Go on with your life with a new enthusiasm, purpose, and dedication. The movie *Schindler's List* tells the story of how a Nazi Party member and wartime profiteer became a savior to more than one thousand Jews during World War II. Mr. Schindler began employing Jews to work in his factory because they provided the cheapest form of labor. He ended up literally buying the life of each Jewish worker he chose to put on his list. Each person on

Schindler's list escaped death and survived the war because of his protection.

As I watched the film and reflected on it afterward, I was deeply moved. I tried to identify the point at which I saw Mr. Schindler make the decision to do everything in his power to save "his" Jews. The scene I settled on as the turning point was when Mr. Schindler was walking toward his shiny automobile in his overcoat on a gray afternoon. The air was filled with ashes, the remains of those who had gone to their deaths in the ovens. The ashes were sifting down from the smoke stacks, ashes of death like so many evil snowflakes, leaving their dark film on everything. Mr. Schindler held out his hand to receive them, then ran his hand across the fender of his automobile, wiping them away. I think this action symbolizes the point at which he decided to save those he could out of the ashes.

At the end of the movie, those Schindler Jews who remain alive today filed past Mr. Schindler's grave in Jerusalem, each one showing respect for the man who chose them by name to be saved from death. I found myself wondering how differently one would live life if she knew her life had been spared in such a way. I imagined it would inspire her to live life fully, with strength of purpose, enthusiasm, and dedication.

We are all like the Schindler Jews in one respect. Christ came into this world—where we were all destined to die without his protection—and chose us individually to live. He risked all, and paid all, to buy each one of us so that we could go on to live fulfilling and useful lives. Paul's letter to the Ephesians describes it this way: "Because of his great love for us, God, who is rich in mercy, made us alive with Christ even when we were dead in transgressions—it is by grace you have been saved. And God raised us up with Christ and seated us with him in the heavenly realms in Christ Jesus, in order that in the coming ages he might show the incomparable riches of his grace, expressed in his kindness to us in Christ Jesus" (Ephesians 2:4–7). Just as the Schindler Jews live out their lives in light of the sacrifice that was made for them, we should be inspired to do the same.

Our inspiration, however, should go even further. Because of God's demonstration of love for us and his faithfulness, we have assurance that we will not end up in the ash heap. Although we may, at times, live through the fires and pass through the cinders and ashes of life, that is not where we will end up! God wants to lift us up out of the ashes, purified and renewed, to go on to experience the "incomparable riches of his grace, expressed in kindness to us."

When you find yourself in the cinders, don't let that become your identity. Hold on to your relationship with God. Offer the cinders of your life as a living sacrifice so you can go on to see God's will for you—his good, pleasing, and perfect will that will lift you from the ashes and toward a happy ending.

FOUR

Everybody's Servant

Trying to earn your keep

CINDERELLA EARNED HER KEEP by doing those dismal tasks nobody else wanted to do. She was disgraced, treated without respect, and forced to serve those around her. Perhaps she thought she had to do this in order to keep her place in the family and make sure she wasn't abandoned. Perhaps she doubted anyone else would have her. Or maybe she looked at herself in the mirror and believed the degrading comments of her stepsisters and stepmother, doubting anyone could love someone as soiled as she had become. Maybe she forgot how much her father loved her as a child, before she could do anything to earn his love.

Whatever the rationale, Cinderella was a slave in her own home as long as she had to do what she did to earn her keep. As long as she feared losing her place, as long as she feared she might not measure up to the expectations of those she tried to please, Cinderella could not escape being a household slave.

Cinderella's slavery ended when she accepted the love the prince offered her. When she married him, she became a princess, an heir to the kingdom and was graced with favor by the royal family. Can you imagine what a disgrace it would have been if, after being elevated to her new position of freedom, she tried to earn her keep by scrubbing the palace floors? This is, however, what many women do when they try to earn their keep, both with God and with people, after being freed by God to become his heir. Living a life of slavery after God has freed you is a "dis-grace." It disconnects you from the grace of God and keeps you in a form of bondage from which God already freed you.

Any woman who is driven by feeling she must act a certain way to earn her keep with God, her family, or her peers is limited by fears of what might happen if she doesn't measure up to the standards others use to measure her worth. This applies to the career woman who bases her self-esteem on the degrees after her name, the title on her name plate, or the success of her business, as much as it applies to the woman who strives to be the perfect homemaker, sexual partner, wife, and mother out of fear she may lose her husband's love. It also applies to the woman who legalisti-cally adheres to the rules of her religion in an effort to stay in God's good graces.

Do you believe your value is inborn, or do you continually strive to prove your worth? Are you confident God loves you even when you aren't perfect, or do you relentlessly try to earn his love? Do you freely express yourself, or do you try to do whatever you think is required to establish your value or earn love? The answers to these questions will tell you if you are enjoying the freedom God offers or if you are living in bondage.

The woman who tries to earn her keep runs the risk of being detoured from becoming the woman God created her to become. Striving to measure up to external demands scatters her attention and energy. She cannot follow God's lead while darting around, following the whim of every person she tries to please. And by suppressing the best that is within her, she may end up living a life that has little to do with her talents, desires, and abilities.

I'VE HAD EXPERIENCE TRYING to earn my keep with God and people. My first response to God's love was a simple welcome. I didn't come from a religious family. I knew I had nothing to offer but my simple love and acceptance of what was being offered. But after several years of being a Christian, I began to feel the weight of outside expectations.

I had studied the Bible enough to know the kind of life a Christian should live. I knew my life should be characterized by freedom from sin. But while I felt quite comfortable with how I measured up in most areas of my life, one area that was out of control was my eating. Throughout high school and most of my college years, I struggled with compulsive overeating. The harder I tried to get my eating under control, the more out of control it became.

My junior year in college I asked God to use my life to draw others to experience his love. One night, while I was praying about this in the dorm, my friend Gabriel Ferrer called me. He asked me to come to a retreat with him and give a talk to a group of college students. He said he had been in a quandary over who to ask to help him since accepting the invitation to speak. As he had prayed that day, God had brought me to his mind. I eagerly agreed to help.

This is my chance to be a leader, I thought, *to teach others about God.* The opportunity seemed to call for a new level of dedication, a greater level of service. I thought I would jeopardize my credibility as a leader if I didn't get my eating under control, so I made up my mind: I was going to stick to a healthy diet. I thought such a decision was mandatory if I wanted to honor God with my life.

I then walked to my car and drove to the nearest ice cream parlor where I ordered not one, but two ice cream sundaes. I pretended one was for my roommate, took the two sundaes with me, and parked in the alley behind Swenson's while I ate them both. Afterwards, I panicked. What did this mean about me? I wanted to please God, to live the life of freedom he promised, to prove to those who saw my life that God brings freedom. Something must be terribly wrong.

Every day that passed before the retreat I grew more apprehensive. I didn't feel worthy to tell anyone else about God when I obviously couldn't control my life. I tried to think of something to say in my talk with the young people who would be attending the seminar; I prayed God would lead me, speak to me, help me, even get me out of this speaking engagement. I kept gravitating toward the Scripture that said, "Those who belong to Christ Jesus have crucified the sinful nature with its passions and desires" (Galatians 5:24).

Great! I belonged to Christ, but my flesh was alive and passionately eating everything it desired! How was I supposed to speak on that Scripture? I gave up. I said, "Okay, God, I know better than to try to pull that one off. What more do you want? I'm working hard here trying to be a good Christian. I'm trying to follow all the rules and use everything I have for you, but I can't crucify my old nature with its passions and desires. The harder I try, the more I want to eat, and the more weight I gain. I give up." The fact that I gave up on using this Scripture didn't mean I wasn't planning to speak at the retreat; it just meant I didn't have a clue what I was supposed to say.

When the day came for the retreat, I asked Pat to come with me for moral support. As Gabri, Pat, and I drove toward the mountain conference center, I was strangely quiet, dreading that I was about to disappoint my friend and make a fool of myself. About two hundred college students had shown up for the retreat. Walking into the large meeting room, the three of us stood out in stark contrast to the group: We were Caucasians, and they were all Asians. I mention this only because I had been hoping I could disappear, or at least be inconspicuous. But that, obviously, wasn't meant to be.

Gabri was scheduled to speak for the morning session, and I was supposed to speak in the evening. I still had hope that God would give me some clue as to what I could say without feeling like a total hypocrite. You see, my inability to control my eating made me feel disqualified, but I was too embarrassed to talk to anyone about it. I didn't know what to do.

In the morning session, while Gabri was speaking, I began having severe pains in my abdomen and side. I tried to make it through Gabri's talk, but was overcome by the severity of the pain. I doubled over and asked Pat to take me outside. As soon as we were out in the cold mountain air, I could stand up, but the pain persisted. Pat steadied me.

"Pat, I'm going to faint," I said.

"No, you're not going to faint . . ." He didn't get to finish his sentence. I fainted.

From my perception, I was suddenly unconscious of the pain but very much conscious of the presence of the Lord. From Pat's perspective, I was just unconscious. He interrupted the meeting to get Gabri and appeal for help. So much for being inconspicuous!

I may have been unconscious of this world, but I was clearly conscious of the Lord. Then it seemed the Lord finally spoke to me: "Connie, apart from me you can do nothing. You can't stand up apart from me. Your next breath, your every breath, is in my hands. Apart from me you can do nothing. Do you understand?" He made it clear that he didn't want some nice little gift package of my good deeds. He wanted me, all of me, as I was, complete with imperfections and extra pounds. I was utterly unaware of Pat's and Gabri's frantic efforts to revive me. God had my full attention.

"Okay, Lord, take me. Take me." I said these words out loud.

That was all Pat and Gabri heard me say after I fainted. The words sent them into a panic. Thinking I meant for God to take me from this life, they became genuinely afraid. They argued with my prayer, saying, "Lord, don't take her. She doesn't know what she's saying."

When I regained consciousness, Gabri and Pat were shaking me and slapping me, while someone tried to arrange for medical help. Gabri frantically prayed for my quick recovery, since he wasn't prepared to give another talk that evening. (And he thought *I* was!) They lifted me off the icy ground and helped me to a bathroom, where I became violently ill. When I came out, I was shaking convulsively, obviously in no condition to walk. The two of them carried me to a cabin and covered me with Gabri's heavy sheepskin jacket and several sleeping bags. I continued to shake violently. Medical help was out of reach. They prayed for me until the pain subsided enough for me to fall asleep.

When I awoke several hours later, the sun was going down. I was utterly exhausted, helpless, wrung out. I picked up my Bible and opened it to the Psalms. I don't recall if I looked up this particular psalm or if I happened on it, but this is what caught my eye in Psalm 116:12–13, 15. King David wrote, "How can I repay the LORD for all his goodness to me?" This was what I had been asking myself. I thought I had to give God a life that was a perfect example of goodness and self-control. What could I give God to repay his goodness? The answer startled me: "I will lift up [or take] the cup of salvation and call on the name of the LORD."

Then the psalmist said these words, "Precious in the sight of the LORD is the death of his saints." I had previously thought this meant that it was precious to God whenever one of his saints died because they went to heaven. Now I saw this verse in a different light, in the light of the other verse I'd avoided as the theme for my lesson: "Those who belong to Christ Jesus have crucified the sinful nature with its passions and desires." God didn't want my good deeds; he wanted me to yield my entire being to him. He wanted my self-efforts to die, so that I would receive the life of Christ and live out the life to which he called me by his supernatural power.

Another Scripture passage fell into place: "I have been crucified with Christ and I no longer live, but Christ lives in me. The life I live in the body, I live by faith in the Son of God, who loved me and gave himself for me" (Galatians 2:20). Wow! God didn't want me to do anything to impress him or the people to whom I would speak. God wanted me dead, dead to my own efforts, alive to him. For the next hour or so I wrote down passages of Scripture as they came to mind and made sense in this new light.

If God found the death of his holy ones precious, I was a precious sight that night when Gabri and Pat came to check on me, because I looked like death warmed over. I was very weak, but I told them the Lord had given me a message to deliver. They helped me to the dining room, where I managed to eat a few bites before the evening meeting.

There was very little energy left in me, but the Lord came shining through. My presentation was nothing to speak of, and my delivery was weak, but the message and the power of God were strong. I told the congregation that God had explained to me that he doesn't want our performance; he wants us. He doesn't demand our perfection; he gives us his. There is nothing we can give to the Lord for all he's done for us. All we can do is receive the cup of salvation, praise the one who continually gives us everything we will ever need, and lovingly cling to the one who gives us life. Apart from God we can do *nothing*, but we can do *everything* through Christ who gives us strength!

I have never, before or since, seen such a powerful response as I saw that evening in that group of people. God was speaking to his people. It was staggering to realize that it is God's desire to give us the power we do not possess so that we can deal with the areas of life that hold us in bondage. We all ended up on our knees, weeping and singing tremendous songs of praise. Lives changed dramatically that night as people repented of trying to earn their keep with God and simply took the cup of salvation he offered them because of his gracious love.

God's steadfast love is not something you can earn. He gives it only as a free gift. It is an offense to God, a "dis-grace," to try to earn what you could never afford anyway, what God wants to lavish on you out of his unmerited favor and love.

DESPITE LEARNING MY LESSON at that mountain retreat center, I have continued, at times, to try to earn my keep with people. When I was at the church I wrote about in the last chapter, I worked very hard, not only to please God but to earn the approval of those who were the standard-keepers. But life is complicated, and people are unpredictable. I discovered that no matter how hard you try to earn your keep with people, no matter how hard you work to earn a place of ongoing acceptance or prominence, you can't manipulate and control the reactions of others.

In the end, when the church leaders chose to remove me from my position of ministry, their decision had nothing to do with my performance. My performance was excellent—no one doubted that. But when my husband's fall threatened the image the church leaders wanted to portray, when the issues raised threatened their level of comfort, all I had done to earn my keep didn't matter.

The process of losing my position was certainly devastating, but it was also very enlightening. Instead of busying myself with external role-playing to various audiences, I was left alone, without a position, without a title, without so much as a job to earn my keep in even the most basic terms. I was at home with my daughter, Casey, and new baby, Taylor. Then eighteen months later I had another baby, Haley. I felt disoriented. I had previously gained my sense of self-worth from my work and relationships with my peers. Now I was in a new city where I knew no one and no one knew me, and my husband was working fifty to sixty hours per week. I had plenty of time to think through the adjustment I had to make—whether I liked it or not! The process was difficult, but I found unexpected freedom in not having to please people. I also learned one of the most valuable lessons of life.

When I had no way to earn my keep with God or with people, I found I didn't have to anymore. I discovered, perhaps rediscovered, that God loved me for me, just me, the person he created. I had become so used to working hard to please God and others that I had lost sight of the stunning truth that God loves me for who I am, not for what I do or fail to do. God loves me. Period. Nothing can change that.

In addition, even though I wasn't fun to be around, I had no status, and I didn't even have enough money to go out to lunch, I discovered some true friendships that endured during this time of loss. I've found nothing more precious in this life!

Finally, I made a choice to live life on a new basis and judge it by new criteria. No more worrying over what people thought or constantly striving to meet higher and higher externally imposed demands! Instead, I began to play at life, secure in the knowledge that there was no way I could lose God's love. What multiplied joy and productivity has followed!

The letter to the Galatians addresses the issue of how to live once you embrace the freedom God offers. "Make a careful exploration of who you are and the work you have been given, and then sink your teeth into that. Don't be impressed with yourself. Don't compare yourself with others. Each of you must take responsibility for doing the creative best you can with your own life" (Galatians 6:4–5 THE MESSAGE). When you stop trying to earn your keep, you are free to discover what God has put within you and free to express it as creatively and enthusiastically as you can. You don't have to prove yourself to anyone. On the basis of trusting in God's unshakable love for you, you are free to do whatever you want to do.

While discussing this issue with my sister, Velma, she said she wished she knew her purpose in life the way I seemed to know mine. I asked her what was closest to her heart. I already knew from her life what her answer would be, for she has a gift of loving and expressing concern for others, especially her little grandson, Derrick. Yet, even though loving and caring for others is what Velma is most enthusiastic about, she didn't think taking care of Derrick was as significant as what other women were doing with their lives.

That way of thinking was keeping her in bondage. I encouraged Velma to realize that her love for our family and her influence on her grandson are worthy pursuits. Giving herself wholeheartedly to the tasks close to her heart is service to God as valuable as anything any other woman chooses to do.

When our sense of self-esteem is protected by the assurance that God values us and what we do, and when we know his love will never change, only then can we find courage to express ourselves freely. We will start living to please God and not people. Our fear of people's reactions will diminish. When we stop looking to others to validate our lives, their disrespect will no longer destroy us.

LET ME GIVE YOU one more example. My son, Taylor, and his friend Timmy were playing upstairs in Taylor's bedroom while I chatted with Timmy's mom downstairs. Suddenly, we heard a loud scream. Timmy shot down the stairs and ran past us, out the front door. Taylor came stomping down the stairs, obviously angry. Tears streamed down his red cheeks. His teeth were clenched, as were his fists. He plopped himself down on the stairs and let out a wail.

"Taylor, what happened?" I asked.

It took Taylor some time to choke out the words. "Timmy . . . Timmy . . . Timmy ate my artwork!"

Timmy's mom and I started laughing. "He did what?"

"It's not funny!" Taylor glared at me as though I had betrayed him.

"Okay, honey. That just sounded funny. Tell me what happened."

Taylor marched back upstairs and returned with a piece of white paper with some sort of drawing on it. Across the top of the page his teacher had written "Peanuts grow on vines in the ground." Taylor had colored the bottom half of the paper brown. The vines above the ground were colored green. He had glued peanuts on the brown part of the paper to show how peanuts grow underground. Above the vines he had written "10" followed by "TAYLOR" followed by the numeral "5."

Pointing to the paper he said, "See, I made this artwork. I wrote all the letters of my name right. And I put a "5" because I'm five years old. And I put a "10" because I counted ten peanuts." Then he started to cry again.

I sat next to him on the stairs and counted the peanuts on his paper. There were only nine peanuts and one small hole where I assumed the tenth peanut had been. "Taylor, do you mean Timmy ate one of these peanuts?"

"Yes, I was showing him my artwork, and he just grabbed it and ate it. Then he threw the shell on the floor, like it was trash."

I realized my mistake quickly, apologized to Taylor, and assured him that I would never treat his artwork like it was trash. I promised him we would repair the damage to his picture, and I vowed to never let anyone eat his artwork again.

While he was at school the next day, I replaced the peanut and sealed his precious masterpiece in an acrylic frame. When he got home and saw how his artwork was protected, he was thrilled. He promptly went upstairs to create more. He drew and colored more than a dozen pictures that day.

When Taylor had looked to Timmy for affirmation, he was rejected. But I love Taylor, and everything he creates is precious to me. When I protected his artwork, he gained a sense of security. Knowing I would protect his artwork gave him the freedom to express himself, and his productivity multiplied—in abundance!

How many times have you held back because someone figuratively "ate your artwork?" Maybe it wasn't a drawing; perhaps it was a shared idea, a part of yourself you opened up to a friend or loved one, your hopes or dreams. How many times have you expressed yourself, looking for someone to affirm your worth, only to have them chew it up and throw what was left on the floor as if it were trash? It doesn't take many experiences like those to squelch true self-expression.

God sees your life as precious, your self-expression as priceless. Be assured that God will never eat your artwork. Instead, his love provides the framework to protect your attempts at self-expression. His love can provide the reassuring security you need after others have degraded what you have shared of yourself.

Likewise, God approves of you. You are free to pursue excellence in whatever you choose to do. As you prayerfully explore who you are and accomplish the work at hand, you can joyfully present your masterpieces to him.

You need not compare yourself to others, but are free to be yourself and bring out the best within you. God doesn't judge us on the basis of how well we do compared with others, but on how well we do compared to how well we *could* do with what he gave us to work with. We don't have to earn our keep with God, and we can't earn our keep with people. What a relief!

We can never count on people to accept and appreciate who we are and the things we do. But with Jesus as our Prince, we don't have to. He has given us his kingdom—not to sweep and scrub and try to earn our right to be there, but to live with him as his bride, a true princess of the kingdom of God.

FIVE

The Search for True Love

Learning that True Love is searching for you!

In the Rodgers and Hammerstein rendition of the Cinderella story there is a twist to the plot that is left out of some of the other versions. Near the beginning of the story, while Cinderella daydreams of her true love, the prince is in his castle, longing to find true love for himself. He doesn't want an arranged marriage to a bride who will love him out of mere duty or lust for his position, power, and wealth. He wants someone to love him for himself. So he dresses as a commoner and ventures out (without the usual fanfare) into his own kingdom in search of true love.

Because the prince was accustomed to the fanfare and the cheers of the adoring crowds along the sides of the road whenever he would emerge from the castle in his royal procession or gilded coach, he took quite a risk by coming out unannounced. We don't know how he was received as he moved through the village incognito, but when he arrived at Cinderella's well he was tired and weary from his travels.

Cinderella greeted him kindly and offered him a drink from her well. She expressed concern that he was so tired and thirsty. He welcomed her kindness along with the drink. He didn't mind her rags, her soiled face, or her work-worn hands as they brushed against his. He saw in her someone who treated him with respect and genuine interest.

Once the prince was satisfied that he could find true love, he headed back to the palace and sent out invitations to a magnificent ball to all the eligible maidens of the kingdom. He knew at least one who would receive his love with genuine affection. When Cinderella came to the ball, and then ran away because she was fearful of being seen in her old rags, the prince had to send out his emissary with a written proclamation to search for her, find her, and bring her back so he could marry her.

When Cinderella was found and taken back to be united with the prince in marriage, she received more than just the love of a husband. In most versions of the fairy tale, Cinderella had lost her father at an early age. She had been longing for a romantic love and partnership, but no doubt her heart still longed for a father's love, too. The little girl inside the young woman hungered for a father's protective care, for someone to watch over her with fond affection.

By marrying the prince, Cinderella entered into a new relationship with the king as well. She became part of the royal family, a daughter to the king, a joint heir with the prince. Her new life in the palace provided her with an intimate relationship with the king and far greater privileges than she had ever had in her limited relationship with her own father.

LIKE THE PRINCE IN this version of the story, Jesus abandoned the glory of his heavenly kingdom and came to earth without his usual fanfare so he could search out those who would truly love him. He didn't want a duty-bound relationship based on the pursuit of his power, position, and privilege. He wanted someone who would love him for who he is and who would receive his love in return.

Jesus too had a conversation with a woman he met at a well when he was tired and weary from a journey. Jesus' friend John tells this story in the fourth chapter of his Gospel. It is the story of a Samaritan woman who spent her life searching unsuccessfully for true love. The woman had come to the well near noon to draw water for her household. Most of the women typically came to the wells to draw water and socialize first thing in the morning, in the cool of the day. It was unusual to draw water at noon because of the scorching heat at midday.

Perhaps this Samaritan woman wanted to avoid the others. She did not have the socially acceptable marriage the culture of her day prescribed. In a time when divorce carried a great stigma, especially for a woman, she had been divorced not once or twice, but five times. And now she was living with a man who wouldn't even marry her. Like Cinderella, the woman Jesus met at Jacob's well was deemed less than worthy.

The Samaritan woman was accustomed to being treated with disrespect within her own community, and the Samaritans as a community were not respected within the nation of Israel. The Samaritans were a mixed race, hated by the Jews as half-breeds, traitors to God and Israel. A Jew would not speak to a despised Samaritan any more than a man would speak to a fallen woman in public. So when the Samaritan woman saw a Jewish man sitting at the well, her best hope was probably that she would be ignored. But Jesus surprised her, probably even shocked her, by speaking. This is their encounter:

Jesus: "Will you give me a drink?"

Woman: "You are a Jew, and I am a Samaritan woman. How can you ask me for a drink?"

Jesus: "If you knew the gift of God and who it is that asks you for a drink, you would have asked him and he would have given you living water."

Woman: "Sir, you have nothing to draw with and the well is deep. Where can you get this living water? Are you greater than our father Jacob, who gave us the well and drank from it himself, as did also his sons and his flocks and herds?"

Jesus: "Everyone who drinks this water will be thirsty again, but whoever drinks the water I give him will never thirst. Indeed, the water I give him will become in him a spring of water welling up to eternal life."

Woman: "Sir, give me this water so that I won't get thirsty and have to keep coming here to draw water."

Jesus: "Go, call your husband and come back."

Woman: "I have no husband."

Jesus: "You are right when you say you have no husband. The fact is, you have had five husbands, and the man you now have is not your husband. What you have just said is quite true."

Woman: "Sir, I can see that you are a prophet. Our fathers worshiped on this mountain, but you Jews claim that the place where we must worship is in Jerusalem."

Jesus: "Believe me, woman, a time is coming when you will worship the Father neither on this mountain nor in Jerusalem. You Samaritans worship what you do not know; we worship what we do know, for salvation is from the Jews. Yet a time is coming and has now come when the true worshipers will worship the Father in spirit and truth, *for they are the kind of worshipers the Father seeks.* God is Spirit, and his worshipers must worship in spirit and in truth."

Woman: "I know that the Messiah is coming. When he comes, he will explain everything to us."

Jesus: "I who speak to you am he."

At this point the disciples came back from getting supplies, and the woman, forgetting her water pot completey, hurried into the city and said to the men there, "Come, see a man who told me everything I ever did. Could this be the Christ?"

The Bible says Jesus needed to go through Samaria. Most Jews would go miles out of their way to avoid going through Samaria, but Jesus needed to go through Samaria. I think he needed to go there because he knew there was a thirsty woman on her way to a well alone—a woman thirsty for love, thirsty for acceptance and a kind word, a woman who had been searching for true love her whole life and had found only rejection and disappointment. She had settled for far less than she had hoped for in life and love. Jesus needed to go through Samaria to offer her more. He personified True Love, and True Love had come searching for her.

Jesus saw everything that soiled the woman's reputation, but that didn't dissuade him. He came with a message: "True love is seeking you." The woman was asking questions about the right way to worship God. Jesus was telling her that the God she sought in her ignorance was secretly there, looking for her to worship him, not on this mountain or that one, but face to face.

The Samaritan woman knew Isaiah's prophecies foretelling the coming of the Messiah: "For to us a child is born, to us a son is given, and the government will be on his shoulders. And he will be called Wonderful Counselor, Mighty God, Everlasting Father, Prince of Peace. Of the increase of his government and peace there will be no end" (Isaiah 9:6–7). She wanted to know the right way and the right place to find him. To her amazement, she learned that he had come looking for *her*. Jesus revealed his secret to this woman, the secret that he was the prince in disguise, the promised Messiah.

Just as with the prince, Jesus also wanted to send out an invitation to every subject in his kingdom so anyone who would love him could come into his palace and dance in his arms. But the love story between God and his subjects was somewhat more complicated by the matter of sin. A debt of sin needed to be paid before any of his subjects would be free to accept his invitation and enter his kingdom. The price to be paid was death. If God were to find the true love he sought, he must pay the debt for the ones he loved—they couldn't pay it themselves.

John tells us this in his first letter: "This is how God showed his love among us: He sent his one and only Son into the world that we might live through him. This is love: not that we loved God, but that he loved us and sent his Son as an atoning sacrifice for our sins" (1 John 4:9–10). Once the debt was paid, all are free to come if they will respond to the invitation. In the very last chapter of the Bible, the invitation is given again: "Come! Whoever is thirsty, let him come; and whoever wishes, let him take the free gift of the water of life" (Rev. 22:17). God has invited us to drink deeply of his love, to have our deepest desires satisfied.

How many times have you, like Cinderella, run away from God when you felt unworthy or feared he might expose your shameful secrets? Like the prince, God too sent out a written proclamation of love, even though he knows our inadequacies. He wants us to know, in no uncertain terms, that True Love is searching for us. Isn't it ironic that many who spend their lives on the often painful quest to find true love may actually forfeit the very love they desire by running away from intimacy (with God and people) out of fear and shame?

I came to understand this concept through my relationship with Patrick. When I first met Pat, I was attracted to his musical abilities. He was singing in a musical at the time (it happened to be *Cinderella*), and his fine voice and stage presence were hard to resist. As we dated over the next two years my love for him grew. While going through premarital counseling, we took a psychological test that compares how you see your partner to how your partner sees him- or herself. Surprisingly, although Patrick knew me almost as well as I knew myself, *my* predictions of *his* reactions bore no resemblance whatsoever to how he saw himself. Apparently, I was in love with the image I projected on him (or he projected) rather than with the man he actually was. The counselor cautioned us to develop the kind of communication and intimacy necessary for me to get to know and love Patrick's real self.

Throughout our marriage, I thought we had that kind of intimacy. I genuinely loved Pat with each passing day and year and regularly told him how much I loved him. I endeavored to make our intimate relationship an expression of the sincere love I felt for him. Still, there came a moment, after six years of marriage, when he lost his ability to receive the love I genuinely offered. After he fell sexually, he felt tremendous shame and self-reproach. Whenever he heard me say "I love you," he discounted it, telling himself, "She loves the man she thinks I am. If she ever knew the real me, she wouldn't love me." He feared I would reject him and leave if I knew him fully. So he kept silent and tried to present the image of a man he thought I could love. All those years Pat forfeited the love he longed for, even though I offered it sincerely, because fear and shame caused him to run away from the risk of rejection.

A wonderful thing happened when Pat turned to face me truthfully, confessing his sin and affirming his hope that we could stay together. His courageous decision to allow me to know him fully gained him a substantial reward. Sure, we had a few difficult years spent reestablishing trust. However, now he can receive my love for him, love that had escaped him before. He knows I love the whole person, not just the image. This has made our friendship and intimate relationship far more satisfying than they were before the crisis in our marriage.

This experience helped me understand our capacity to receive the love God offers us. The Bible makes it absolutely clear that God holds no illusions about our perfection, nor does he require it. We don't have to keep up an image; God already knows all there is to know about us and loves us anyway. When we comprehend God's acceptance of us as we are, we can stop running and turn toward God, finding consolation in his embrace. As God showers us with his love, we become able to absorb it. This kind of encounter with True Love satisfies us to the depths of our beings.

THIS FAIRY TALE ANALOGY is fine and good as far as the story goes, but how can we really know God's love in a way that touches down to the depths of us? How can we have an intimate relationship with someone who walked the earth long ago, someone we can't see, touch, hear, or chat with over lunch?

This is the mystery of faith. Many loved God and knew him before he came to earth, trusting only the promise that he would come. Others throughout the last two thousand years have known him and loved him, trusting in the historical and biblical record that he did come, that he is who he claimed to be. This is the mystery of revelation. If you respond to God's offer of love and love him, accepting him in his disguise as a commoner, then he will reveal himself to you like he did to the woman at the well. Then you too will know Jesus personally, fall in love with him, and live with the assurance that he will never leave you. You will know that he is in you and with you, guiding you day by day. This kind of personal relationship with God through Jesus Christ has been experienced by people around the world, throughout history.

While on a tour of Israel, I had a conversation with our Israeli tour guide, Moshe, about the resurrection of Jesus. One day we had gone into the empty garden tomb, the tomb reported to be the one where Jesus had been buried. And, sure enough, the stone was rolled away, and no one was buried there.

Moshe was not only a tour guide; he was also an archeologist. He was thoroughly familiar with Jesus' claims to be the Messiah, and he knew that Jesus said his resurrection should be taken as proof of these claims.

"Moshe, what do you think of all the historical and archeological evidence for the resurrection of Jesus?" I asked.

"Well, any good student of history and archeology must admit that Jesus lived and died and rose from the dead as his followers said he did."

This surprised me—not that the evidence was there, but that this man, who was not a Christian, would state the fact so strongly.

"Then what do you make of Jesus' claims that his resurrection proved he is the Jewish Messiah?" I asked him.

"I choose to draw no conclusions from the fact that he rose from the dead," Moshe answered. "If I did, there would be religious implications, and I am not religious."

Historical facts do not force an acceptance or even a revelation of who Jesus was and is to the unresponsive heart. To Moshe, who didn't have eyes for the prince, Jesus was just another commoner who happened to have miraculous powers. But to those who are open to what Moshe calls the "religious implications," the reality of what True Love did to win us not only staggers the imagination, it opens our hearts and changes our lives for ever after.

The world looks for true love in glamorous displays of passion; God hid it by displaying it on a cross. In this way he insured that only those truly seeking his love would find it. I still remember being caught by surprise the first time I realized God's true love for me.

My kids and I had decided to get Pat's car detailed as a gift for Father's Day. We had to sneak to use his car without him suspecting anything. We dropped the car off at the body shop and had to wait for a couple of hours until it was done. While waiting, we walked around the area, hoping to find something interesting to do. We ended up walking up and down the aisles of a building supply store (since the surrounding neighborhood wasn't designed to entertain small children).

We happened down an aisle filled with nails of every size and dimension. My son, Taylor, an inquisitive five-year-old, picked up a giant nail, more like a sharp tent peg than a nail. "Mommy, is this the kind of nail they used to nail Jesus to the cross?"

"I suppose," I said. I had never given the matter much thought. "It must have been long and strong to hold a man's weight to a wooden cross." My two girls, Haley and Casey, ages three and nine, were listening.

Taylor's face held a serious expression. "How did they do it? Where did they put the nail?" He held the point of the giant nail to the palm of his hand.

"Well, I'm not sure, but I think they put it here—" I pointed to his wrist—"so the nail would have some bones to hold on to."

Casey made a face that said she was as squeamish as I was about the course the conversation was taking, but Taylor was fascinated. "How did they do his feet?"

"Well, I suppose they put one foot on top of the other and nailed them together."

Taylor put one foot on top of the other and started to wobble. "Didn't he try to get away?" he asked.

"No, he came to die for our sins, so we could be forgiven and live with him forever." I was relieved to turn the conversation back to the religious themes that were more theoretical and less graphic. But Taylor wanted to know how much it hurt and how much blood spurted out and . . .

At that point Casey intervened. "Taylor, stop! You're grossing me out!" She turned to go to another aisle, followed by Haley. Taylor tossed the nail back into the bin and followed the rest of us.

That experience did something to me. It took my breath away to see my only son holding this nail to his wrist, knowing that God's only Son knew a moment when the hammer and spike, flesh and blood and wood came together. It came together not because he had done anything wrong, but only because God so loved the world. At this moment my theological ideas were nailed to reality in a new way.

The realization of God's love hit me again when Pat and I were touring Israel. We missed our tour bus one morning while staying in Jerusalem, so we decided to explore the old city of Jerusalem on our own. We hailed a cab and set out on our adventure.

First, we chose to walk around the city on top of the old walls. To do so, it's necessary to buy a ticket, then climb the ancient stairs to a pathway that winds along the top of the wall, sometimes widening, sometimes narrowing. We met interesting characters along the way: a woman with missing teeth praising Allah while begging with her young daughter, a Christian man from the United States who sits on the wall every day to pray for the peace of Jerusalem, even men dressed in civilian clothes carrying Uzzi sub-machine guns. (These gave us quite a scare because we didn't realize that civilians who had served in the military were allowed to carry military weapons openly.)

As we proceeded, turning corner after corner, not knowing what startling sight we would meet around the next turn, I looked out away from the city. There, not a stone's throw away from me was a hillside that bore a striking resemblance to a skull. The sight stopped me in my tracks.

"What?" Pat asked.

"Look, there's the place, the place of the skull."

We both knew the story in the Bible of how Jesus was beaten mercilessly, forced to carry his cross through the city streets, and forced to climb up a hillside nearby to a place called Golgotha, which means the place of the skull. There on that hillside he lay down on a cross and allowed Roman soldiers to nail his hands and feet to the wood. Those passing by hurled insults at him as he suffered.

I could see it now. If I wanted to, I could yell loudly enough to be heard across the way to the top of that hillside. Below us, between the wall and the foot of the hill, was a road and a bus station. In days of old, those passing between the city and the hill could see the crucifixions taking place. (This was by design. The Romans used public executions as a deterrent against crime.) In that moment I realized in a new way that God didn't just love me in a story. He didn't stay safely in his castle. He came to earth. He climbed that hill. His cries filled the air. His love story was one he didn't just talk about or write about. He lived it.

As Pat and I stood silently taking this in, the Holy Spirit said to me, "He did it because he loves you." Knowing this gives me courage and enthusiasm to express myself and live courageously. I can't fully explain how I know, but I know. And knowing—really knowing—God loves me has had a tremendous impact on my life.

No one has expressed this love better than poet Maya Angelou during her interview with talk show host Oprah Winfrey. When Oprah asked her to describe the most important moment of her life, I fully expected her to say it was the moment she read her poem at President Clinton's inauguration. Instead, she told of a time when she was a young woman. Maya was studying voice with a renowned teacher, who also held spiritual discussions from the Bible. Maya would attend these discussions along with his other students, who she looked up to because many were well-known for their talent.

One day the teacher gave each person in the group something to read aloud. When it was Maya's turn to read, she read "God loves me." Her teacher told her to read it again. So she did. He told her to read it once more. Maya felt that he was embarrassing her in front of everyone in the group, but she repeated "God loves me" once again. Then her teacher told her to try to "know" that God loved her. It was then that Maya realized that she was capable of doing anything good, anything helpful. *That* was her greatest moment. Maya told Oprah that even though that incident occurred in 1953, each time she says those words now she is still filled with gratitude and wonder. They reconfirm to her that she is a giving human being with rights to everything on this earth.

At the end of the interview Oprah reflected back on Maya's comments as if trying to fully grasp them for herself. She repeated the words "God loves me," and thoughtfully stated that knowing that intellectually is different than really "knowing" it. If you truly "know" it, she said, "Your light would be so bright nobody could stand it." She is right.

"DEAR FRIENDS," THE APOSTLE John wrote, "since God so loved us, we also ought to love one another. No one has ever seen God; but if we love one another, God lives in us and his love is made complete in us" (1 John 4:11–12). One other way we know the love of God is to see it lived out in the lives of those who have God's love living in them. Love is more than just a feeling; it is a way of conducting yourself toward others that always involves self-sacrifice.

The Bible describes love this way: "Love is patient, love is kind. It does not envy, it does not boast, it is not proud. It is not rude, it is not self-seeking, it is not easily angered, it keeps no record of wrongs. Love does not delight in evil but rejoices with the truth. It always protects, always trusts, always hopes, always perseveres. Love never fails" (1 Corinthians 13:4–8a). If you see this kind of love in a human life, you have seen God revealed in one who knows him.

I know of one such woman. Edith married late, at twenty-nine, after growing up in Bonanza, Arkansas. Her primary requirement for a husband was that he not be a coal miner, as were most of the men in that small coal-mining community. She entered marriage with the conviction that hers was a lifelong commitment. Edith always wanted a family, and dreamed of children and grandchildren. She was thrilled when she became pregnant. Her subsequent miscarriage at home during her fourth month saddened her deeply. She said it was a little boy. After that Edith couldn't have children, which was a shame because she knew she would have been an excellent mother. Besides, her husband wanted children too.

After twenty-two years of marriage, when she was fifty-one, Edith's husband came home with news no wife can bear lightly. Another woman was pregnant with his child. More than that, he was bringing the baby home to live with them. Edith's family said she should leave him. "The thought of it! How dare he bring home some illegitimate child for you to look after," they said. But she stayed. What's more, she loved the little girl.

Less than two years later Edith's husband brought home a second daughter, born of the same mother. Most women would have walked away or slighted the children in some way—but not Edith. She stayed and loved the girls as if they were her own flesh and blood. She loved them like a mother, although she never had the title. (These girls already had a mother, and Edith would never undermine their love for their real mother or speak against her in any way.)

Edith cooked meals, cleaned up after them, ironed their clothes, and polished their shoes. When the younger one suffered recurrent earaches, Edith sat up all night, rocking her and singing softly, saying over and over again how sorry she was for the pain. She braided their hair and baked their favorite flavor of birthday cakes, never grudgingly but with genuine care and affection. On Sunday mornings she took them by the hand and walked with them to the church on the corner three blocks away. Edith's husband never went with them; he said the church didn't need one more hypocrite in the pews.

When they packed to go to their mother's house, which they did regularly through a shared custody arrangement, Edith often

sent a bag of groceries or a little something special if someone in
the other family was sick or not feeling well. The girls' real mother
had several older children, some who had children of their own.
Edith offered to babysit and treated them all as though they were
part of her extended family.

Never once did Edith let anyone shame the girls or mistreat
them. She loved them simply and continually as they grew up. She
refereed their bickering and tolerated the upheaval of their
teenage years without complaint, even though she was in her late
sixties by then. Throughout her life Edith continued taking care
of them with a steady, unwavering love, sharing what little extra
money she had with the girls whenever they needed anything.

After the girls married, Edith and her husband eventually went
to live with the oldest daughter and her family. When Edith's husband passed away, she lived to become "Granny" to four grandchildren, whom she treasured. One could only wonder at such love.
God knew the two girls had needed her, but it was hard to fathom
how she could give her life so freely under conditions that would
have made most women bitter. Edith's love was baffling in retro-
spect, perhaps especially to me because I was the recipient of her
love, the youngest of the two girls. Edith was my stepmother.

After Dad passed away, I finally asked her what I'd wondered
about for so long: "Edith, why did you stay with Dad after he was
unfaithful to you? Why did you raise us?"

"Well, kiddo (she called everyone "kiddo"), I always wanted
children of my own. In a way, you kids were the answer to my
prayers. Besides, I love you girls like you were my own. You
couldn't help what your daddy did." It was as simple and profound
as that: "I love you girls"! Then she added, "Besides, look how it
paid off. I have four beautiful grandchildren, and your Daddy is
dead and gone. He's missing out while I'm getting blessed."

Granny Edith lived to be eighty-six. When her health was failing, our mother came to help my sister take care of her. Some people would think such a thing strange, but Edith's love was unusual. Mom appreciated the love Edith had shown us and her over the years. She said it was only fitting that she help take care of Edith because Edith had taken care of us when she herself wasn't able. When Edith passed away, Mom and several of her children drove ten hours to attend the funeral. I don't know anyone who knew Edith who didn't love her. They could not help but respond to her love. True love, even in a simple life, is irresistible. Love never fails.

My sister wrote this poem for Edith's funeral as a tribute to her life:

> She viewed the world through eyes of love,
> Choosing only to see the good;
> When wronged, and she was so many times,
> She forgave and understood.
> She expected nothing for herself;
> And gave everything she had
> To enrich the lives of those she loved
> Standing by them good or bad.
> She found her joy in simple things
> Choosing licorice over gold,
> A lady after God's own heart
> A sainted angel to behold.
> She'll live forever in our hearts
> And we'll miss her every day
> But she wouldn't want us saddened—
> She'd say, "Kiddo, I'm okay."
>
> —BY W. ROBIN LOPEZ

I kept one of Edith's flannel nightgowns, like the ones she wore when she sat up all night and rocked me as a child. Whenever I need to remember what true love feels like, I wear it. It reminds me that I was touched by the true love of God even before I knew what it was. It also reminds me that I ought to love others as I have been loved, in simple and tangible ways.

True love isn't the glamorous romance you see in the movies. I've heard it said that people need love most when they deserve it least. I have found that to be true. At our wedding, Pat sang a song to me during the ceremony about how, when two people work through things together, their love is able to "climb the hills" of any trial they may come up against.

The true love of God was expressed when Jesus made his uphill climb to the top of a hill shaped like a skull. His climb ended in the ultimate act of self-sacrifice. And through his act of love, we now have access to God's love that can flow through our lives to others. Whenever we venture to love, we too must remember to follow in the footsteps of Jesus: making an uphill climb to the place of willing self-sacrifice for those we love.

PATRICK AND I have been married fifteen years now. What I thought was just a verse in a song has been proved true in life: True love is an uphill climb. But because I have received the love of God in my life, accepting that fountain of living water Jesus offered the woman at the well, I have a source of love in God. His fountain of living water refreshes me during love's uphill climb.

Whenever human relationships fail, when those I depend on to love me are unwilling or unable, God's love never fails. I think this is why Edith could love us as she did. She had a source of love in God and knew how to access the love he put within her. As I learn to rely on the fountain of God's love, human relationships are no longer a desperate attempt to find someone to love me perfectly. Instead, God's love fills me up. His love springs up within so I too can offer his living water to weary travelers I meet along the road of life.

SIX

All the Eligible Maidens

*Daring to be yourself and join
in the dance of life*

CINDERELLA READ THE INVITA-
TION: all of the eligible maidens in the kingdom were invited to
attend the ball. She knew she was one of the eligible maidens, but
ridicule from her mean-spirited stepsisters caused her to doubt
herself. "Surely the prince didn't mean maidens like her!" they
said. They pointed to her position as a mere scullery maid, her
poverty, her filthy rags. When she tried to make herself over by
creating a suitable dress for the ball, they tore at her dress,
destroying it and her hopeful self-confidence.

Cinderella accepted their attack on her worthiness as if it
were the truth. She gave up. She no longer dared believe that she
was eligible to go to the ball. She allowed her stepsisters to disqualify her from pursuing her dream of dancing with the prince.
Although her dream was waiting to come true, she almost missed
it by believing her stepsisters' lies.

• • •

WHEN PATRICK AND I married the summer before our senior year in college, we were rich in love, rich in friends, and rich in happiness. Our financial situation was another story. All we could afford to drive at the time was a compact Opal station wagon. When a hit-and-run accident took the driver's side door off at the hinges, we didn't have insurance to repair the damage or money to fix the car properly, so my dad took Pat to the city dump in search of a door that would fit. They found a door for that make and model that fit perfectly. Unfortunately, the door was red and the car was white. Since we didn't have another option we could afford, we decided to drive our white Opal station wagon with one red door and save our money to replace the door or the car as soon as we could. As time went on, the novelty wore off, the jokes died down, and we almost forgot that our car was unusual.

That year many of our friends finished college and got married, so wedding invitations were numerous. We became accustomed to spending our weekends attending bridal showers, bachelor parties, weddings, and receptions. When our friend Gabriel Ferrer invited us to his wedding to Debby Boone we thought nothing of accepting the invitation and looked forward to the wedding without any hesitation.

That August day dawned bright and clear. The congregation attending the ceremony was divided into the brides' guests and the grooms' guests. It was only as we followed the procession from the church to the Wilshire Country Club that a different kind of distinction came to our attention.

There we were, in our pitiful little white Opal station wagon with its red door, locked in this procession of vehicles with more than your average share of Jaguars, BMWs, Mercedes, Rolls-

Royces, Bentleys, and limousines. We couldn't help but laugh at the situation and our own naivete. If we had given the situation some forethought, we could have borrowed an appropriate car, but we hadn't. So we blushed and giggled, shook our heads, rolled our eyes, and laughed some more. We stopped laughing, however, when we turned into the gates of the exclusive club and realized valet parking was the only option.

As we inched along the drive, we prayed the other guests wouldn't notice us. Ed McMahon stood on the curb chatting with another man. I could just imagine him telling Johnny Carson about the little white car with the red door, and I didn't want to be a joke in Johnny Carson's monologue. I just wanted to wish my friends well on their wedding day and celebrate their happiness.

A sense of shame threatened me. I felt that sinking feeling in my gut like I used to feel when other kids teased me because of the wrecks my dad had driven. How many times had I begged Dad to drop me off two blocks from school so I wouldn't be embarrassed? Now, without thinking, I had driven into a situation of far greater contrast. These people were obviously eligible to be here; by appearances, we were not. When our turn came to exit the car, we dashed out as quickly as we could.

Once a safe distance had been achieved between ourselves and the offending car, we could laugh again. Although there were more than a few celebrities among the guests, we were at ease. We knew we were invited guests with as much right to be there as anyone else. When we saw Gabri and Debby, they welcomed us and thanked us for coming. We enjoyed the beautiful music and the lavish buffet, chatted with those we knew, and shared in the joy of seeing our friends get married. We took our time and planned our escape, trying to avoid as many eyes as possible. Not many other guests saw us leave, and we had fun pointing and laughing at the valet driving such a funny little car.

When it was all over, Pat and I agreed that we had wanted to go to our friends' wedding reception, and our friends wanted us to celebrate with them. It would have been a loss on both sides if we had talked ourselves into believing we weren't qualified just because of our little white car with the red door.

LIFE IS GOD'S CELEBRATION and we are all invited to feast at the buffet table. Some of us appear more or less eligible than others if you only look on the outside. But God knew that when he invited us, and he invited us anyway! We are all eligible! If we believe the lie that we are disqualified to lead the life God has invited us to enjoy, we will miss out.

People may have all sorts of reasons for telling you that you are not eligible to live the life you long to live. Some love you but want to spare you possible disappointment and embarrassment. Others—like the ugly stepsisters—are jealous and mean-spirited and try to hold you back for their own advancement. Still others are simply unable to see who you are in all your glorious potential. They speak what they see to be the truth, but they don't have the vision to see that you are eligible for the life to which you aspire.

I once helped my daughter's second grade class with a project designed to teach the children to identify their dreams and then work toward achieving them. The children enthusiastically began talking and drawing pictures of the many hopes and dreams hidden within their hearts and minds.

Later the teacher and I were surprised to hear that a few parents were upset. One mother wrote, "I don't think it is right that you stir up such hope in my child's mind when he will only be disappointed. Then I have to explain to him that he can't have what he's dreaming of." The only way I can make sense of such a statement is to assume the woman who wrote it has known disappointment and is trying to protect herself and her son from further disappointment.

Anyone who tells you that you're not eligible is projecting his or her own fears onto your life. The real danger, if you listen to these messages, is that although you may be spared disappointment, rejection, or embarrassment, you will also miss out on your own fulfillment and the joy of living. Your response to people with this message should be to appreciate their good intentions, thank them for their concern for your welfare, and then disregard what they have said.

Just as every Cinderella story has cruel stepsisters, each person has someone in her life who plays the stepsister role at one time or another. This is the person who tears you down, ridicules, threatens, and demeans you with the goal of holding you back. He or she is jealous, envious, selfish, insecure, vindictive, and hateful. Often those who fight most viciously against you need to tear someone else down to feel better about themselves. When dealing with people playing this role, you must consider the source and remind yourself that their attack on you says more about them than it says about you.

The last group of those who would disqualify you are those who lack vision. They are like the snickering parking attendants who couldn't see how people driving a car with one red door could really be invited guests. You can't blame them for their conclusions regarding your present circumstances, but you need not believe their pronouncements about your future either.

Even Jesus had to deal with those in his own family who couldn't see who he was and what his life was meant to accomplish.

Although Jesus' brothers loved him, they didn't believe he was the Messiah. They challenged him to go up to the Feast of Tabernacles and prove himself to the doubting mobs and religious leaders who vowed to kill him. But Jesus didn't let their limited vision limit his life and fulfillment of his purpose. He didn't lash out at them or try to make them acknowledge what they could not see. He simply let them go on to the feast without him. Then he went on to do what he came to do, knowing that one day they would see and believe. We would do well to follow his example when dealing with those who lack God's vision for our lives.

You may discover, as Cinderella did, that those who try to disqualify you don't know the real person hidden within you. When you press on to experience the life God intends, your detractors may not even recognize you, just as Cinderella's detractors didn't recognize her at the ball. Then again, they may have a sudden change of heart. You may find, as Jesus did, that when you live out your life to its intended conclusion and have fulfilled your purpose, those who lacked vision before may come to believe in you and cheer your success. They may eventually even take credit for helping you succeed! Hold on to the vision God has of you and be willing to follow it. Stop listening to those who try to hold you back, whatever their motivation may be.

Every woman is invited to join in the dance of life, to experience the honor of living life to the fullest. Every woman is eligible to become the woman God dreamed of when he created her. The surest way for any of us to miss the ball is to believe we are not one of the eligible maidens. Then we may give up seeking our dreams, act as though what we once longed for doesn't matter any more, or simply try to avoid remembering the hopes we once held dear. Even Cinderella mumbled something about not really wanting to go to the ball. "I suppose there will be other times," she sighed. But in her heart she knew she cared more than she dared admit.

Don't listen to the voices around you that say you are disqualified from the dance of life or from enjoying the buffet of worthwhile relationships and experiences God has for you. They may be the voices of father or mother, sister or brother, boyfriend, teacher, employer, husband, or so-called lovers who tell you you're not eligible for the life you long to experience. It may be your own inner voice negatively comparing yourself to other women or some unattainable ideal. It may be a thousand voices speaking through the media saying that the eligible maidens are more beautiful, more confident, more intelligent than you are. Any voice that tells you you're not one of the eligible maidens is the voice of your enemy or of one who cannot see the truth.

MY DAD DIED WHEN I was twenty-six, three weeks after I gave birth to his first grandchild. Ours was a tumultuous relationship, mostly because Dad was a tumultuous person, and this affected all his relationships. I could grieve my dad's passing with a calm sorrow because I knew he loved me and he knew I loved him, and because he had lived long enough to see the baby.

His death was terribly unsettling. He had always carried tremendous aspirations and had worked incredibly hard to provide for his family, trying to succeed in various business ventures. When the funeral director asked what he had done for a living, we laughed. You name it, he did it at one time or another, or so it seemed. He was always building something in the garage, remodeling kitchens, selling his latest creation of carpentry. In the long run, however, his hard work and busy genius didn't amount to much in terms of material success. I can't say whether it was his tendency to move from one venture to the next before any business had time to be established, or if it was his anger that interfered with business relationships, or if it was his addiction to gambling that dwindled away his hard-earned dollars. What I do know is that he died without enough money to bury him.

My sister told me how panic-stricken he had become when, in the midst of a heart attack, he realized his financial situation. As he waited for the ambulance to arrive, while racked with pain, he made Edith get the newspaper so he could show her an advertisement for a cremation service. It must have broken his heart to realize his life had come to this. It broke mine to think of him being cremated—not that there is anything wrong with cremation if that is what the person chooses, but because he wanted to be buried and in his last hours succumbed to the fact that he couldn't afford it. Daddy died that night. We never got a chance to tell him that we would make sure his body would be buried as he had wanted.

I prayed about all of this because it troubled me so. I knew my dad had a relationship with the Lord, so I didn't worry about his final destination. I was more disturbed with how his life ended up. In this state of mind I had a dream: I was back in the house where Dad, Edith, my sister, and I had lived from the time I was three until I was eighteen. It was a few days after Dad's funeral, and it had been years since any of us had lived in that house. I had gone into Edith and Dad's bedroom to sleep with Edith because I didn't want to be alone. I had often done this when I was a little girl. She was glad for the company and the comfort of having me close. We heard loud noises coming from the living room: The front door opened and someone was clambering around, whistling loudly, and knocking into things.

Edith and I looked at each other with curious wonder rather than fear. This kind of noisy clamber was very familiar. Dad was always barreling through the house making lots of noise; whistling loudly was his trademark. Before we had a chance to investigate, the hall door opened, then the door to our bedroom swung wide.

There stood Dad beaming proudly. He wore a clean, plaid flannel shirt and work pants. Around his waist was a tool belt filled with new tools, the kind used for carpentry work.

"Dad, what are you doing here?" I said. "You ... I mean, aren't you ... well, aren't you dead?"

"Why, of course I'm dead. Don't you think I know when I'm dead?" He shook his head with a triumphant little laugh, implying that he couldn't believe how little I understood. When he was alive, he would have been angry and insulted, but now he seemed happily free from that. "I know I'm dead, but I just had to come back to tell you something. I finally found a place where they appreciate me! They know what I'm worth up here. Yep, they know what I'm worth. You see these tools?" He shifted his weight proudly. "The Lord's letting me work on the mansions. I just had to let you know, they really appreciate me up here!" Then he left, whistling loudly and happily.

It does my heart good to think of Dad up there working on my mansion, whistling and working without the destructive forces within and the other interferences that had robbed him of success in his work here on earth. I'm not saying this was necessarily a message from my dad. It may have been my own mind's way of trying to make peace with disturbing emotions. However, this dream stirred up other thoughts that enhanced my understanding of life. It made me wonder what kind of difference it makes for a person to know, here and now, what my dad seemed to discover in heaven: that we are truly appreciated by God, valued highly and considered worthwhile. How differently would we live and work if we knew with confidence that God has a job for us to do in keeping with our talents, interests, and abilities? I believe it can make a world of difference.

In my dream this sort of contrast was implied. Dad never came out and said, "No one on earth believed in me or fully appreciated my talents or saw my worth." He didn't have to say it. By saying God believed in him, appreciated him, and knew his worth, the contrast was obvious. People really don't affirm others the way they need to be affirmed. Instead, the voices we typically hear are the voices of other people who tend to tear us down. We don't always hear the voice of God as clearly as Dad, in my dream, seemed to hear it once he was free of this world.

Each of us must choose who and what we will believe. Depending on your source of feedback, you will see yourself as either debased and worthless (at least worth less than others) or as useful, valuable, and worthwhile. The day-by-day choices you make about which voices you will believe set the course your life will take. If you believe you are not eligible, you will never reach your dreams or become all God created you to become. You will give up or slink away in shame when challenged or derided. You will miss all the good things in the buffet of life that God has prepared especially for you.

But if you believe God made you for greater things and has a purpose for your life, you will not settle for being held back. You will find the courage and determination to overcome whatever stands in your way. Believing God's view of you opens the door to the good things he promises, the good life that he dreams you will lay hold of and that he wants you to live.

God's word states clearly that everyone's life has purpose. He expects us to believe his Word and work diligently toward our freely chosen goals. When we fall, we must choose to believe what God says about us rather than believing the voices that say our bad behavior proves we are not eligible for the good life God has for us. We must believe we can change and courageously continue to work toward change, regardless of our setbacks. First, we walk by faith, and then (as a result of believing we do have purpose) God will cause his good will for our lives to unfold.

When Pat was publicly removed from his position as youth pastor, he was firmly committed to providing for his family. The only job he could find was working as a waiter. As part of his side duties, he had to clean the toilets in the restaurant. Every time he cleaned the toilet he couldn't avoid the voices in his head reminding him of where his sin had led him. He talked with me and our friends about how hard it was to go back to such menial work. His friend, Larry, gave him some tapes by Zig Ziglar from his *How to Stay Motivated* series. Thereafter, Pat listened to Zig's words of encouragement while he swept floors and cleaned toilets.

"You are where you are, you are what you are because of what has gone into your mind," Zig said. Pat could affirm that was true. Zig went on to say, "You can change where you are, you can change what you are by changing what goes into your mind." Pat determined to defy the voices that said the good purpose of his life was destroyed.

Time and again, our friends Rayna and Larry and I would remind Pat that his confession of sin guaranteed God's forgiveness and cleansing from all unrighteousness. This wasn't easy for Pat to believe because the consequences were so painful and his circumstances pointed out his fallen position. However, he chose to persevere in faith. He chose to keep listening to Zig who said, "If you don't like you the way you are, don't worry! You are not stuck with you the way you are. You can change!" Pat listened to voices that echoed the word of God and he lived as though what God said was true. This kept him from giving up even though it was terribly hard to go on.

MAYBE THE REASON SO many of us feel as though we are missing out on the purpose we sense God has for us is that we are waiting for *him* to do something, while God is waiting for *us* to do something. Those who don't prepare themselves by starting in faith to work toward their goals may very well miss their noble purpose in life.

Abraham Lincoln is one of my heroes. A quote from Lincoln startled me into thinking about the importance of preparing for the great future God has planned for us. Early in his life, before any of his later successes, Abraham Lincoln wrote these words: "I will prepare myself, and someday my chance will come." Here was a great man whose greatness had yet to be made known to his generation. His belief that God would have some great purpose for his life prompted him to prepare himself for useful service.

After he had prepared himself, when our nation was in great need, perhaps God looked around and said, "Now, who do I have that is prepared to be used greatly in this time of national crisis? Ah, yes, here is a man who has prepared himself for the purpose I have for him."

How might the course of history have been altered if the young Abraham Lincoln hadn't believed he had a great destiny, or had believed but had failed to prepare himself? How might the future course of *your* life and the future of those you may touch be changed if you believe that God has a great purpose for your life and take action to prepare yourself in the hope that someday your chance will come? You will know the answer to that only if you dare to believe and let that belief prompt action.

What kind of action? You will discover the particulars if you take time to pray and think about what you believe your talents and purpose might be. Then pursue whatever good direction you want to pursue. Following are some general ways to prepare yourself.

Look for opportunities to make a positive impact on the lives of others, wherever you are and whatever you are doing. Pat didn't stay cleaning toilets for very long. His good work and genuine concern for doing an excellent job as a waiter caused him to be promoted to headwaiter. From there, he went back into restaurant management and continued to do an excellent job, although it wasn't his idea of what he wanted to do with his life. He trusted that if he were faithful to do his best where he was, the day would come when God would lift him up and help him find a more noble purpose. Whatever work you do, do it to the best of your ability as though you are doing it for God himself, and you will be promoted.

Continually work to develop your talents, skills, and abilities. While I was out of work, I didn't just sit home and feel sorry for myself. (Actually, I did feel sorry for myself!) I also learned to type and to use a computer and a word processor. I did this in hopes of making myself more marketable in a field other than youth ministry, trusting that God could use me somewhere. Do something to develop new skills and abilities in order to become better prepared to express your God-given talents.

Educate yourself with the goal of providing a useful service. I knew that one day I wanted to be useful to God through writing and public speaking, so I took writing classes through community education programs. I also enrolled in seminars for public speaking. Educate yourself with a goal of moving toward something you would one day like to do that would provide a useful service. Even if you are far from your ultimate goal, take small steps to start educating yourself now.

Sift through criticism to find any useful bits of truth, and then throw away the rest. Some criticism can be helpful if it helps you to see how you can change for the better. If you find no redeeming value in the criticism, if it is condemning rather than corrective, toss it.

Work hard and persevere. Pat and I have both had to work hard over the last several years. We worked hard at work, at our relationship, at being good parents, at holding on to faith that God does have a good purpose for our lives. It does take hard work and perseverance to live as though your life has a noble purpose, especially when circumstances seem to say the opposite. It takes perseverance to believe the still, small voice of God while living in a world where the voices telling us we are not eligible are shouting loud and clear.

Sociologists say that "you will see yourself the way you believe the most important person in your life sees you." This observation shows how we let others influence our self-concept. I struggled for years with feelings I was somehow soiled, in a lower class than most girls and women when it came to my appearance. In a speech class a few years ago, I was asked to create a three-minute speech relating to a magazine ad. The ad I chose showed a bride dressed in a white wedding dress and veil. The caption read, "Now is your moment to be beautiful."

The ad reminded me of a time when I was about five years old. My dad had taken me shopping for an Easter dress. I remember seeing a rack filled with white lace dresses made for first Holy Communion. They were the most beautiful dresses I had ever seen.

"Oh, Daddy, please can I have one of these dresses?" I begged.

He gave a quick glance at the dresses and said, "No, little girls like you can't wear white."

I don't know if the dresses were too expensive, or if he was being practical because my favorite pastime at that phase of life was making mud pies. Whatever his grown-up reasons, my little-girl heart registered the message: "Little girls like you can't wear white." To me those white dresses represented all that was beautiful.

Perhaps this early experience of how I believed the most important person in my life saw me helped create my later insecurities. Perhaps it influenced me to choose a wedding dress that was ivory rather than white for my wedding. I don't know. What I did know when I looked at the bride wearing white and telling me, "Now is your moment to be beautiful," was that I had a choice to make.

By rethinking my childhood belief from a more mature perspective, I realized that my dad would never have told me I would never be beautiful. He regularly told me how pretty I was and affirmed me in many ways. Instead, I had misunderstood his comment and assigned meaning that was not intended. I didn't react to what he meant; I reacted to what I believed he meant. By gaining fresh understanding and changing my mind, I was ready to accept the possibility of beauty that my previous misconceptions had withheld from me.

If you see yourself the way you believe the most important person in your life sees you, your self-worth will be subject to that person's moods, whims, and misperceptions. But you can change your self-concept by challenging beliefs that may not be correct. You can also make a dramatic shift in your self-concept by simply changing who you allow to play a primary role in your life. When you make God the most important person in your life and meditate on how *he* sees you, your sense of who you are will undergo a dramatic transformation.

You will begin to see yourself in a far more positive light. God appreciates you much more than you appreciate yourself. He knows what you are worth and proved it when he paid a priceless ransom to buy you for himself. And he stands ready, offering his hand to you, inviting you to join him in the dance of life.

Listen to the muffled desires of your own heart. God may be the one who planted those desires within you. God made you a unique person. He doesn't want you to change to be like someone else. You may have pushed aside your true desires for self-expression while you were busy trying to be what others thought you were or should be. If so, you may have to quiet yourself in prayer and reflection to find these hopes and dreams. But when you accept who God made you to be and begin to pursue your heart's true desires, you can start to enjoy life as the divine celebration it should be.

Do you want more out of life? Dare to admit it. Dare to hope, and then prepare for the life you long to live. Dare to dream of becoming the person you hope you can be. You don't have to pretend life is one grand party at every moment. Obviously, it isn't. But when you face your problems and character flaws, humbly asking God for help, he may surprise you by changing your pumpkins into magnificent coaches and your rags into beautiful gowns.

God says you are eligible. Dare to live as though you believe it too. If necessary, wrestle with unbelief. There may be a part of you that doubts your eligibility for the good life, but there is also a part of you that knows you were designed with a purpose. Wrestle with whatever you must, but don't stop until you believe!

Take hold of the opportunities life presents with an sense of expectancy. Enjoy loving your family and friends. Enjoy learning and growing. Enjoy each season of life. Enjoy the adventure of solving your problems. Enjoy all the blessings God provides— food, beauty, sex, color, fragrance, laughter, work, creativity—in whatever unique forms he provides them. Enjoy pleasing the God who created you and loves you.

God longs to show you off at the dance of life. And when you catch the vision of his dream for you and truly believe that you are one of his eligible maidens, you're already on your way to the ball!

SEVEN

Dry Your Tears—You Can't Go to the Ball Looking Like That!

*Changing into the woman God created
you to become*

CINDERELLA HAD TRIED to make herself over to look more like the eligible maidens, but when her stepsisters tore up her homemade gown, leaving her dress destroyed and her hopes in tatters, she gave up. She wasn't ready to go. She was left weeping alone in the garden, while those who tore her down left for the palace looking beautiful and worthy of the invitation.

When the fairy godmother appeared, she assured Cinderella that she would go to the ball, but she didn't send her off in rags and a tear-stained face. Instead, she used her power to transform Cinderella into Ella, the beautiful maiden. Ella wasn't someone new; rather, she was the full expression of the beautiful woman hidden beneath the cinders, wounds, and exhaustion of Cinderella's servitude.

We too may look at ourselves and rightfully conclude that we can't make it to our dreams in our current condition. It's good to know God never intends for us to remain in the condition in which he finds us. He created us with the happy surprise of transformation designed into our being.

I've heard it said, "God loves you just the way you are, but he loves you too much to let you stay that way." In a loving relationship with God, who accepts us unconditionally, we do not have to be transformed to gain his acceptance. But transformation is how God brings out the best in us.

The transformation I'm talking about is not a superficial change in appearance or behavior. It is not modeling yourself after the fashions of others or pressing yourself into some mold you think others will accept. Outward changes may be the easiest to make, but outward change without inner transformation is bogus; it doesn't last. It's like one of those miracle weight loss plans that causes you to quickly lose weight that you can't keep off. How many times do we need to try to make ourselves over from the outside before we realize that outward changes are not what we truly long for in our hearts?

The transformation I'm talking about is a metamorphosis: a marked or complete change of character, appearance, and condition. It is a change of substance that takes place inside and changes everything on the outside. Such transformation is no mere New Year's resolution; it takes place all the time, but seems to happen by magic, as when a butterfly emerges from the cocoon where a lowly caterpillar hid.

Dare you hope for such a change as this? Dare you aspire to change into the full expression of the woman you long to be? Yes! Have faith, you can change to become all the woman God created you to be.

In the Disney movie, Cinderella's stepmother and stepsisters leave for the ball without her. As she rushes out to the garden, drops to the ground, leans against a bench, and begins weeping with her face in her hands, the refrain from the opening song begins to play . . . "No matter how your heart is grieving, if you keep on believing, the dreams that you wish will come true."

Cinderella says, "Oh no, it isn't true. It's just no use, no use at all." She sobs. "I can't believe, not any more. There's nothing left to believe in, nothing."

Meanwhile, we see the approach of a swirl of sparkling lights that turns into Cinderella's fairy godmother. She seats herself on the bench, cradling Cinderella's head in her lap. The fairy godmother says, "Nothing, my dear? Oh, now, you don't really mean that."

"Oh, but I do."

Her fairy godmother says, "If you'd lost all your faith, I wouldn't be here, and here I am."

Even though Cinderella didn't think she had enough faith to believe she could make it to her dreams, she had faith she didn't even know she had—and so do you.

It doesn't take tremendous faith to be transformed. It takes only a glimmer of faith, if that faith is placed in one who has power to transform you. Your glimmer of faith may be an irrepressible longing for a better life; it may be an inner conviction that life can be much more than it is, that you are created with a purpose you have yet to discover and fulfill; it may be a whispered prayer for something of which you dare not speak to others because you have tried to change so many times without success.

Transformation starts with that glimmer of faith and the desire to move out in search of what you hope for. The Bible says, "Now faith is being sure of what we hope for and certain of what we do not see" (Hebrews 11:1). If you have the desire and a glimmer of hope for the life you cannot see, you have enough faith to be transformed.

Let me use an illustration adapted from one our pastor used recently. Suppose two families live in a secluded area, separated from town by a river over which there is a bridge. The river sometimes freezes during the winter. A woman from the first family is deathly afraid of going near the frozen river because as a child she fell through the icy cover and almost drowned. Now suppose that in the wake of a powerful storm, the child of the woman who fears the river becomes deathly ill, needing immediate medical attention. Phones lines are down. Her only hope is to get to town and summon help in person.

The mother drives her four-wheel drive vehicle to the bridge and finds it destroyed by the storm. To save her child's life, she must dare to cross the river that appears frozen. She's afraid to try to make it across in her weighty vehicle, so she inches her gloved fingers out on the ice to test it. Slowly, she slides her body out from the bank, fearing that the ice will crack at any moment. She sees the town on the other side and risks all in hopes that she may reach her destination and fulfill her mission. Slowly, fearfully, and painfully, she makes her way across to find the help her child needs.

Now suppose a woman from the other family finds herself in the exact same situation. She too needs to get across the river to bring help for a sick child, but she has never fallen through the ice. She approaches the damaged bridge in her four-wheel drive vehicle. Seeing that the river appears frozen, she drives across the ice to the other side without giving it a second thought.

If the river were not completely frozen, the woman who was thoroughly confident would have drowned just as surely as the woman who seemed to have no faith. Since the river *was* frozen, the woman who had no faith made it across as safely as the confident woman. My point is this: It is not the strength of your faith that gets you where you long to go in life; it's the strength of that in which you *place* your faith. If that in which you trust has the strength to hold you, you will make it. If that in which you trust is faulty, you won't make it. How strongly you feel one way or the other isn't a determining factor. Simply put, faith is a belief that prompts action. Faith must be placed in one strong enough to transform you. When you follow God's lead in the dance of life, you can persistently move beyond whatever obstacles keep you from that which you most deeply desire.

The Bible says that when you delight yourself in God, he will give you the desires of your heart (Psalm 37:4). This doesn't mean that you tell God what you desire and he automatically gets it for you. It goes deeper than that: He actually inspires the true desires in your heart that will lead you to become all he created you to be. Then, when you take your deepest, most heart-felt desires to God and pray according to his will, the power of heaven goes to work on your behalf.

If Cinderella had not gathered the raw materials for her transformation, no amount of the fairy godmother's magic would have changed her life. Just as transformation was not something the fairy godmother did to Cinderella, transformation is not something the Holy Spirit does to you. God will not transform you against your will. Those who go around casting spells on people, changing them into another form against their will, are workers of evil. God always respects the free will he created as part of your being.

Your transformation comes about in the context of an ongoing love relationship with the living God who knows you, knows your aspirations, and knows the latent talents he created within you. As you grow and change, God is with you, ready to take you to a higher level in your development. This cooperation with God is part of the dance—moving together with him, following his lead, agreeing to changes he longs to make in your life.

IT CAN BE SCARY to hope for transformation because once you clearly envision the transformation you hope to see, it is painful to live with something less than what you hope for. Maybe this painful part of the process is what discourages us from hoping and dreaming and praying. I know well the pain of daring to hope for transformation and of struggling under the weight of a reality far removed from that which I longed for, prayed for, and deeply desired.

While growing up, I always knew without a doubt that my mother loved me dearly, but Mom was an alcoholic. In my mind she was like separate people: my real mom who loved me, and the drunk lady who took my mom away and hid her somewhere so I couldn't reach her. When the drunk lady came out, I was afraid of her, embarrassed, angry, and confused. I hated that she ruined our holidays and kept me up all night. Most of all, I hated the confusion I harbored between the love I had for my mom and the anger and hate I had for what alcohol did to her.

One of my prayers took precedence over all others: "Lord, please free Mom from alcoholism." Each time I hoped and prayed, I was sure God would answer my prayer. Then Mom would call me, drunk and cussing and spewing her sorrows, and my heart would break all over again.

When I was in tenth grade, I took up drama and enjoyed getting lost in the characters. Auditions came up for the comedy *You Can't Take It With You*, and I amazed my classmates with my portrayal of one of the characters, a drunken actress who ends up passed out on the couch. They didn't know that I had seen that scenario more times than I cared to remember. The director asked me to audition for the part, but I refused. I knew Mom would want to come to any play I was in, and I couldn't bear to hurt her. The auditions came and went. Laurie Christy got the part of the drunken actress, and I was relieved.

But when I prayed, I felt like God was speaking to me, telling me that I was supposed to play that part. Although it was a moot point, I resisted even the idea of it. I would have to come too close to the feelings I was trying so hard to avoid. Since there was no chance of my getting the part, I told God I would have been willing to do the part if I had it to do over again.

To my surprise and consternation, when I went to drama class the next day the director asked me once again if I would accept the part of the drunken actress. It seems that Laurie had had a change of mind and dropped out of the play. Okay, so God had taken me at my word, and whether I was fully willing or not, I realized he was doing something here that I dare not walk away from. I told the director I would take the part.

Every time I rehearsed the part, each moment I was truly in character, I could think of nothing but how it must feel to be my mom, to be trapped in this clouded existence. I didn't tell my mom what part I was playing, only that the part was funny. I had prayed Mom wouldn't want to come to the play, but she was planning on coming opening night.

The day of the performance Mom sprained her ankle and couldn't come after all. Although I was sorry Mom hurt herself, I was greatly relieved that she wouldn't see me acting like her. I still wondered what God was up to by putting me in this situation, so I approached opening night with curiosity and expectancy. The slurred speech, the staggering walk, the studied attempt to not appear drunk, and the lack of control were the surface actions of a method actor. But as I got into the character, trying to feel what she felt and play the part from that source, God showed me what he had been after.

As I stumbled across the stage and collapsed on the couch, and the family tried to hide me from visiting guests by draping a cover over me, I felt it. I knew what it was like to be inside the drunkenness. I felt the shame as the audience laughed. Now I understood. I had always hated Mom's prison of alcoholism from the outside; now I had a glimpse of how she must hate it from the inside. For the first time I saw how her prison of alcoholism was causing her to suffer. From that moment on, I prayed with new compassion.

THE HOPE I HAD for my mom's transformation was hard to bear. I was scared to think I might be disappointed. Before the play, I had tried not to acknowledge how deeply I longed for her to be free. I had tried to convince myself that if that was how she wanted to live, then it didn't matter that much to me. Now I realized that no one could really want to live that way; she only settled for it because she saw no way out. I dared to admit to myself and to God how very much I wanted my mom back—not the drunk lady, but my real mom who was hidden away somewhere inside the alcoholism. Admitting how much it meant to me made my heart ache all that much more.

Mom moved away to South Dakota, so I didn't see much of her the remainder of my high school years, but I continued to pray for her freedom. My faith in God was growing, and I often talked about God to my family members. Once when I was talking to my oldest sister, Joann, she stopped me. "If your God is so strong, there is only one thing I want to see him do," she said. "I want to see him stop Mom from drinking. Then I will listen to you talk about God. Until then, I don't want to hear it." She had a good point. Why shouldn't the Almighty be able to answer the one prayer that was most important to us?

I confessed to Joann, "I am praying, and I believe, I really believe, that God can stop Mom from drinking." I think she must have seen my sincerity or my fearful hope, because she stopped being defensive and tried to shelter me.

"You know, Connie, I wouldn't get my hopes up," Joann responded. "God can only change those people who want to change, and I don't think Mom wants to change. I don't want to see you set yourself up for a disappointment." I didn't want to admit it, but I was afraid of the same thing.

Mom kept drinking, and I kept praying on into college. As the years passed, my prayers turned into plans. Mom had moved to Eugene, Oregon. I planned to go up to see her over Thanksgiving my freshman year. I had played it all out in my mind how I would share with her God's love and his power to change her life. She would listen and accept his love and have her life transformed. Not seeing her for some time had allowed me to generalize her drinking into the abstract, which made it much easier to continue praying.

When Thanksgiving break arrived, I took the train north for the twenty-hour trip to Oregon. When my sister Diane picked me up at the train station, she looked worried.

"What's wrong?" I asked.

"Mom's drinking. It's pretty bad."

During the drive to her house, Diane and I talked about praying for Mom. She said the same thing Joann had said: "God won't make you change unless you are willing to change." I knew that, but I also knew from my experience on the stage that there was a part of Mom, however beaten down, that *did* want to change, even though we saw no indication of this.

All talk of hope and faith caught in my throat as we drove up to Diane's house. I heard Mom before I saw her.

A vulgar stream of curses was being screamed and muttered loudly. She was staggering back and forth in front of the house next door, looking back toward Diane's house, yelling something about being kicked out. Then she turned and tried to walk away. Mom knew she wasn't welcome in Diane's house when she was drunk, so she was heading for our cousin's house a few doors down the way. We watched as she tried to walk, fell, and hit her head on a car parked at the side of the road. She crawled along on the wet grass, still cursing and screaming. We continued to watch her as she regained her footing (such as it was) and staggered on. She pounded on the door of our cousin's house, but no one answered.

When we went inside, we called down to our cousin's house. Mom wasn't welcome there in her drunken condition either. She had been offered a ride home earlier, but had refused. I watched her struggle to open the door of a car parked at my cousin's house and fall into the backseat. There was nothing I could do.

When I saw Mom the next day for Thanksgiving, she didn't remember anything that had happened or how she ended up sleeping in the car.

Diane told me she had taken Mom to the doctor, who had diagnosed diabetes. He also said that between the diabetes, her smoking, drinking, and poor nutrition (she didn't eat when she drank), she was in dangerously poor health. My mother was standing at death's door at the age of fifty-three. She could easily be dead within six months if she didn't stop drinking immediately. She might not live long enough to see me graduate from college, get married, and have children. After the weekend, I headed back to school determined to pray, terrified that the deepest desire of my heart might be buried along with my mother.

My faith had been whittled down to a tiny speck, but I still believed that God was strong enough and that this prayer was valid. I also had faith that Mom didn't want her life to end that way. I left the matter in the hands of God. I called Diane when I got back to my dormitory and she said Mom wanted to talk to me. That was a good sign. If Mom was in Diane's house that meant she wasn't drinking. Mom got on the line and said, "Hey, baby, pray for me. I stopped drinking, and I'm gonna need God's help." What could I say? Of course I would pray!

I held my breath every time I talked to Mom, fearing that she may have started to drink again, but days and weeks and months passed and she stayed sober.

I spent the next summer with Mom, praying now that God would draw her to himself. Miraculous happenings were taking place in my life that summer. Mom watched in amazement, but with little apparent interest in developing her own relationship with God. I was invited to speak about what God had done in my life to a youth conference hosted by a local women's group. Mom was so proud of me and wanted to attend, although she felt uncomfortable in such a large group. She sat near the back as I told my story. At the end I invited anyone who wanted a closer relationship with God to come forward for a prayer of commitment. Many people came to the front, but my eyes were on my mom seated in the back. Oh well, maybe I was asking for too much too soon.

When we were in the car on the way home, Mom said to me, "Honey, my legs were hurting. Could you and I pray that prayer together when we get home?" And so we did. Then we stayed up late into the night talking. I had my mom back! My prayers had been answered.

Later that night Mom told me how she had accepted Jesus as her Savior when she was sixteen, but fell away when those close to her made fun of her and ridiculed her faith. She told me that when she heard the doctor say she might die, she prayed for God to help her stop drinking, and he did. Hers was a tiny little prayer, voicing her feeble hope for transformation. It was prayed from a most desperate situation, when anyone you asked would have told you there wasn't much chance of transformation. But Mom put her tiny glimmer of faith in the One powerful enough to change her. She reached out toward what she hoped for in life and found herself being carried along toward the life she truly desired. God transformed her life so that she could become the woman he created her to be.

God freed Mom from alcoholism and gave her back to us, gave us the good years we have known with her in the eighteen years since she stopped drinking. Mom was there to share in the joy of my wedding, she stayed with me after the birth of each of my three children, and she helped me learn to be a mother. She has lived to attend my children's birthday parties and to know and love her grandchildren.

My husband and children have never met the drunken lady who used to steal my mother away. The kids only know her as Grandma Goodie—an apt name because like all proper Grandmas, she keeps goodies stashed away for them, gives them too much candy, and bakes them cakes. She has lived to develop her talent for handicrafts, stitching hand-sewn quilts and embroidering her love into dishtowels and tablecloths adorning the homes and lives of her children, grandchildren, and great-grandchildren. She is my biggest fan, our family historian, and a most faithful encourager. She has been there for me to cheer my success when times were good and to offer her support when times were bad. All of this because we dared to hope in the power of God to transform lives.

Last year we planned a surprise seventy-first birthday party for Mom in April. When she suffered a heart attack in March, we were afraid she might not live to enjoy her party. Our family was gathered at the hospital, waiting for her to come out of surgery, when, from our waiting room, we saw a beautiful rainbow arch its way across the sky. Just then the surgeon came in to tell us the surgery had been successful, and that Mom was doing well. The rainbow reminded us all that God is a keeper of promises. It reminded us that the One who can shine his light into an overcast day and transform the sky into a canvas of astounding colors can do the same thing when his light shines into a darkened life—if it is met with just a glimmer of faith.

On April 17, 1994, Mom lived to celebrate her birthday with all six of her children, all sixteen of her grandchildren, twelve great-grandchildren, assorted spouses, in-laws, and friends. More than sixty of us gathered at my home to celebrate her life and the abundant love she has given us over the years. In truth, that celebration was a celebration of the transforming power of God.

MOM'S CHANGED LIFE SERVES as potent encouragement that God can transform anyone who sincerely seeks him. But not everyone's transformation is as dramatic as Mom's extraordinary one. In fact, for most of us it is in the ordinary areas of life where the changes we want to make elude us. Let me give you an example from my life.

As I went through counseling over the past several years, I realized a troubling pattern in my life. While I continually busied myself trying to rescue and care for others, I didn't take care of myself. I neglected myself in almost every important area of life: medical care, personal grooming, wardrobe, physical fitness, and keeping my home in order. Desire for change stirred within me. I admitted this desire to God, my confidantes, and myself, and then turned it into a specific prayer that God would help me learn to take care of myself.

Even though I was ready to change, I soon realized that this pattern in my life was not something that would change by my own willpower. Frankly, my resistance to doing what seemed to come naturally to others baffled me. By reading extensively and writing books dealing with codependent behavior, I learned how growing up in an alcoholic home contributed to these tendencies. I knew I couldn't unravel all the threads woven into my life that contributed to my pattern of self-neglect, but I knew God could change me if I asked for his help.

Then I began to take the simple steps necessary to change in these areas. I gave myself permission to spend time taking care of my personal needs. I decided to invest in my own life, making specific commitments to take medicine on time, wear makeup, have my nails done, update my wardrobe, establish order in our home, and get in shape physically. It is an ongoing commitment. I still pray for God's help with these desired changes, and I also pray that he will change me within so that these outer changes are genuine expression of what he is doing within me.

Day by day, this way of living is becoming more and more a part of me, a true expression of my new nature. The changes are progressive. I am far from perfect in any given area, but I have changed for the better in each area, and people notice. When we sent out a Christmas card with a family portrait, we received more than one comment about the changes people could see in me. Friends from college called to say how beautiful I was—well, how beautiful the whole family was, but they were obviously shocked at the change in me.

Yes, God has made quite a transformation in my life. Isn't it wonderful to realize that God cares about the changes we would like to make regarding how we treat ourselves and live our daily lives? Let him embrace you and lead you as you see changes in these areas taking place.

Over the years I have formed principles about how transformation takes place in our lives. These principles are evident in Cinderella's story, as well as in my mom's and my own. They can apply to your life in both extraordinary and ordinary situations.

Transformation begins with surrender, not self-effort. True transformation is not something you work at with your own strength any more than a caterpillar would design and attach its own wings. Just as the caterpillar surrenders to the cocoon and rests in the assurance of what it will become, we need to curl up into God's loving plan for who we are and who we will be. Psalm 37:4–5 (NASB) says, "Delight yourself in the LORD; and he will give you the desires of your heart. Commit your way to the LORD, trust also in Him, and he will do it." The literal translation of "trust" means to "roll off onto" God. I like that image: rolling your life and future development off onto God, resting in him, waiting patiently for him to transform you.

Transformation comes by acknowledging your true desire for change. If you've tried to change many times, you might be afraid to hope again. But transformation will not begin until you at least acknowledge the unfulfilled desire within you.

Transformation comes by committing the specific changes you desire to God in prayer. When you pray, acknowledge your inability to change on your own, along with your willingness to do what is necessary to change. Ask God to give you strength and guidance to move toward the changes you desire. Your prayers don't have to be eloquent, just honest, specific, and reliant on God's power.

Take simple steps toward transformation. Day by day, take steps toward the desired changes you and God agree are necessary to transform you into the woman he created you to become.

Thank God regularly for the transformation taking place in your life. While you take steps toward your new way of life, don't forget that you do so by the grace of God.

NO ONE NEEDED to convince Cinderella that she had to be transformed before she could go to the ball. Likewise, no one has to convince most of us that we need to change to get where we want to go in life. We will never be perfect this side of heaven, nor does God expect us to be. But although we can't be perfect, we can be fulfilled at each stage of maturity.

Dare to believe you can reach your dreams, even if you need to change dramatically to do so. Take the glimmer of faith you have and act on it. God will shine his transforming light on that little glimmer and change you into all he created you to be.

EIGHT

God Desires Your Beauty

Challenging the belief that you are not beautiful

FROM THE MOMENT CINDERELLA entered the ballroom, the prince desired the beauty he saw in her. He wanted her for his bride. If he had known her hesitations, her family situation, her lowly position, her broken heart over the loss of her father, and the abuse endured in her family, he would have told her it didn't matter. He would have done everything in his power to convince her that life with him would make her forget all of that. And he would have done his best to convince her she was worthy of that life.

Cinderella probably discounted the prince's proclamation of love. After all, the beautiful maiden at the ball was so far from the everyday person Cinderella saw herself to be that even her family members didn't recognize her. Could the prince love a girl who sat among the cinders night after night? Yes! He did love that girl, and he had loved her from the moment he had seen her at the well. And yet he wanted more for her. It seemed so much more appropriate for her to dance with him, openly displaying her beauty.

God has seen each of us at our worst. He knows our shame. He keeps our darkest secrets in his heart. Yet God loves each one of us for who we are. He wants us to get past our losses, shame, and limitations. He loves us too much to watch us live out our days in the dirty rags that characterize our past. This is what the prophet Isaiah referred to when he wrote, "The LORD has anointed me . . . to bestow on them a crown of beauty instead of ashes" (Isaiah 61:1, 3). As I have grown in my relationship with God, one of the constant themes of our relationship is my growth toward accepting the beauty he wants to bring out in my life.

A GARDENING CATALOG FROM the Michigan Bulb Company arrived at our home one afternoon in February. The pages were filled with brilliant photographs of flowers: tulips, gladiolus, Canterbury bells, lilacs, wildflowers, stargazer lilies, painted daisies—pages and pages of growing beauty. I was drawn in by the variety, by the wonder of how such beauty could be expressed in so many different ways. Every page surprised me with the unique design of a different flower.

Since our family was preparing to move into a new home, I allowed myself a leisurely thirty minutes to imagine where the flowers would grow in our now-empty flower beds. The temptation to linger a while longer increased because a floral centerpiece my husband had given me reflected the beauty of the pictures in the catalog, encouraging me to enjoy the moment.

My daughter Casey arrived home while I was looking at the flower catalog. She was captivated. She had never seen so many different kinds of flowers, or at least she had never taken time to notice their unique beauty. Together we chose the flowers we wanted to plant in spring, summer, and fall. I filled out the order form, mailed it, and started to throw the catalog away.

"Mom, can I have the catalog?" Casey asked. "I just want to look at all the flowers for a while." She kept looking at that catalog day after day, discovering new flowers she liked, commenting on how pretty they would be when we got them, drawing my attention to particular flowers, their colors and patterns. The more she looked at the pictures, the more eager she became to get our flowers and get them planted in our yard.

As I enjoyed Casey's enthusiasm over anticipating the shipment of flowers, I suddenly realized that Casey was expecting a shipment of *flowers* just like the ones in the catalog. But we were going to receive a box of flower bulbs. No flower bulbs had been pictured in the catalog. This didn't surprise me, because flower bulbs are ugly. Besides, gardeners are expected to understand that beautiful flowers grow from unattractive bulbs. But little girls don't know that.

Casey has never done any gardening. Her experience with flowers is limited to seeing flowers planted in pots at the local nursery, growing in a neighbor's yard, or arranged in a bouquet at the market. Suppose I don't tell Casey anything about what to expect when her anticipated flower shipment arrives, and she receives her box of knobby little bulbs. She might react in many different ways. She could feel defrauded and angry and throw the bulbs away, or she might hide the bulbs in a drawer so no one would see how ugly her "flowers" were. If she were in a mood to make the best of the situation, she might have fun decorating the ugly bulbs with puff paints and glitter glue. These options all stem from the fact that she does not know that beautiful flowers are hidden within the ugly bulbs and that those bulbs need special care to bring out their innate beauty.

If I explain to Casey that we will receive flower bulbs corresponding to the flowers we chose from the catalog, her response would be entirely different and have different results. She would know to expect a box of bulbs and wouldn't be dismayed by their appearance. She may even have an added sense of wonder that she could be part of the process that turns ugly bulbs into the beautiful flowers she picked out in the catalog. When the bulbs arrive, she would learn to plant them at the proper time, in the appropriate way. She would be able to enjoy planting the bulbs, nourishing them, and waiting patiently for the day the stem breaks through the ground and the blossom she dreamed of so long ago appears.

What you believe about the bulb determines what you do with it, and what you do determines whether or not you experience the potential beauty God created within it. In like manner, what you believe about your inherent beauty will determine what you do with yourself. And what you do with yourself determines whether or not you will ever experience and enjoy the full expression of the beauty God created and hid within you.

Just as the gardener must understand the growth process and participate in the creative miracle that transforms an ugly brown bulb into a brilliant yellow tulip, so, too, you must understand God's growth process and participate in the creative miracle that transforms you into the woman God created you to become—the woman of his dreams. It is faith in the flowers that inspires us to dig in the dirt, to wait patiently for the season that will bring the blossoms.

I READ WITH INTEREST results from a poll of American women who were asked if they thought they were pretty. Eighty-seven percent of the women polled said "no." If these figures are reflective of the truth, that means only thirteen of every one hundred women dare to say they are pretty. Yet our society places such emphasis on physical beauty that women spend billions of dollars each year on beauty products, continually striving for some measure of beauty while continually confessing our perceived lack of beauty.

When I was asked to speak at a women's retreat on the theme "Becoming All the Woman God Created You to Be," I asked the woman who was organizing the event to take a photograph of each woman at the time she registered. Some women resisted having their photos taken, and all were curious about how we were going to use the photos, but most of the women agreed to be photographed. At the beginning of each session during the retreat, we presented a slide show featuring photographs of each of the individual women while a soloist sang a song entitled "Who Am I?" The song was posing the question, "Who am I, God, that you call me by name and love me the way you do?"

At first you could hear and see the discomfort the women felt as they saw themselves on the screen. They laughed nervously, made self-denigrating remarks, and groaned. But in the course of listening to the message of the song and seeing the beauty in the smiles of other women, a change took place. We repeated the song and showed new slides four or five times during the weekend so that everyone could be featured. By the end of the weekend, the nervous laughter was replaced by quiet tears. Everyone at the retreat sensed the realization that we were beautiful to God—perhaps far more beautiful than we ourselves realized. Perhaps it was even possible to put aside our feelings of inferiority to other women in order to appreciate the unique beauty found in each one of us.

I didn't know these women before that weekend, yet I saw beauty in each smiling face on the screen. As I watched the slides,

I tried to imagine God's view of each woman, knowing the beauty he created there and yet watching the women cringe at their projected images. I was surprised that women who looked beautiful to me expressed embarrassment at their appearance.

All the while, my tension mounted because my photograph hadn't been shown yet. I wondered if I could look at myself on the screen and accept what the song was saying—that I too was precious and beautiful in the eyes of God. I had shared with these women stories of my struggle over my self-image and my appearance. They understood. When my picture appeared, the women broke into an encouraging round of applause. At that moment I caught a glimpse of myself through God's eyes. Just as I had seen the beauty in each of the other women, I could see this woman on the screen had a beauty all her own, and she was me.

Can you honestly say you are beautiful without cringing? If not, who convinced you that you're not beautiful? People see only the outside; they don't see the beauty hidden within you—the beauty that glows when you are at your best physically, mentally, emotionally, and spiritually, when you are expressing your talents and creativity. If you listen to these people, you will give up and hide yourself away. Forget them! Forget their misconceptions about you! Instead, consider the possibility that you may be like a bulb that has yet to blossom. Unless you nurture yourself and treat yourself with the expectation of beauty, you will never know how beautiful you can become.

Here are some things you can do to acknowledge and bring out the beauty within you:

- Try to recall the last time you believed in your beauty.
- Remind yourself that what you see may not represent the true depth of beauty within you.

- Remind yourself that there may be far more to you than you now realize.
- If you can't honestly believe in your beauty, try to believe in the possibility of beauty hidden within, like the beauty of the flower hidden in the bulb.

I know how difficult it is to focus on beautiful possibilities if you are held back by shame about your appearance or surroundings. As I reflect on my life, I see the hand of God working steadily to bring me to accept the beauty within me and to dare to nourish it. I can see now that God desired my beauty all along. When I couldn't see anything beautiful in my life, he led me into situations that stirred up my desire for the beauty I had cast aside in my despair. He would not relent until I came to understand that who I appear to be is far less than who I actually am. I now realize that great beauty can be seen as I express who I am. Great beauty can be seen as you express who you are, too.

IT TOOK SOME IMAGINATION to find beauty in my childhood home. We had bought the modest three-bedroom home when I was three. It was situated on a corner lot across from Lakeside Jr. High in a middle-class neighborhood in Southern California. Early on, the large backyard held a swing set and a doughboy pool. There were rose bushes, calla lilies, and we had plenty of lawn for playing childhood games and hiding Easter eggs.

By the time I reached junior high, however, the modest beauty of our home was gone, buried under stacks of lumber and shelves filled with the makings of some brilliant invention as yet unappreciated by the buying public. Dad suffered a sunstroke at some point in my childhood, and after that we couldn't reason with him. His hard work as part carpenter, part eccentric inventor, part handyman, and part entrepreneur lost any rational direction. He filled up our garage with power tools, our patio with building supplies. Our entire backyard looked like a cross between a lumberyard and a junkyard; there was barely a path to walk through. When he filled the yard up to the level of the six-foot fence, he built extensions all around so he could pack in more. It didn't matter to him that we were the laughing stock of all the kids of the neighborhood or that neighbors regularly reported him to the authorities for creating an eyesore and a fire hazard.

We also had six cats and five dogs of various sizes who came indoors to live when there was no longer room for them outside. It was nearly impossible to keep our home in any semblance of order. My stepmother tried continually to keep the place clean, but it was a losing battle. I learned to breathe through my mouth to keep the stench at a distance. What I didn't learn was how to order my surroundings in pleasant ways or create a place of beauty or serenity at home. By the time I reached junior high and had to attend the school across the street from our house, my primary goal was to keep anyone from knowing that I lived where I did.

By then Dad had bought an ancient red truck that looked like a cross between a 1940s fire engine and the truck driven by the Beverly Hillbillies. He needed more space, since the backyard, and now the side yard, were filled to overflowing, so he built six-foot plywood walls around the bed of his monstrous truck and would constantly load and unload it in front of the school, whistling loudly all the while. I went out for every sport available so I wouldn't have to cross the street to go home when most of the kids were leaving school.

I fought hard to distance myself from the disarray all around me. I groomed myself well, dressed as best I could on my small allowance, and looked for any way I could find to keep my identity separate from my surroundings. The summer before eighth grade my sister Diane invited me to spend the summer with her. I jumped at the chance, hoping to find out who I was apart from the clutter in which I lived. I could just be me. No one where she lived knew how I lived or what my family was like.

Diane lived in a two-story apartment complex built around a swimming pool. The pool became the social center for the teens in this small community, and the opportunity to explore my identity couldn't have come at a better time. Puberty had been kind to me. My body was changing in amazing ways, much to the pleasure of the boys around the pool. That summer I learned the power that comes with being physically attractive. I saved my money from babysitting, bought more nice school clothes, and went back to face the eighth grade with assurance that I was far more beautiful than the environment in which I had been raised.

Eighth grade was great! My newfound confidence increased my favor with my peers. I was chosen as a cheerleader and participated with honors in every sport. I had every reason to expect that if I could make it through the year, things would be much easier socially when I graduated to high school. The high school was miles away. No one would have to know what my home was like. I could keep up the image I needed to be accepted.

The summer between eighth and ninth grades, I began to suddenly gain weight. I had always been thin as a child, too thin. But in the course of that summer I went from a weight of 105 pounds to 150 pounds on my 5'1" frame. When I began high school, the kids from the other schools had no way of knowing this wasn't the real me, and the kids who had grown up with me couldn't believe the sudden change. Boys who had fawned over me just last year now looked at me with curious disdain. I was furious!

I was the same person. Why was I being rejected just because my body had played a cruel trick on me?

If my parents had been alert or had had the financial means to take me to a doctor, they would have discovered I had developed a thyroid imbalance during puberty. Meanwhile, I was struggling with this new image of myself as fat and unattractive. I had expected a shipment of flowers only to discover I had received a box of ugly bulbs. No one explained to me that I would grow through this stage. I thought I was supposed to be beautiful, and now I was held captive inside a bloated body.

I reacted by trying to hide myself. I began using drugs more regularly. I had experimented with marijuana along with many of my friends during eighth grade, and now I started smoking pot every day on the way to school, at lunch, after school. My hard-earned wardrobe didn't fit, so I had nothing decent to wear to school. My father's schemes weren't producing the income we needed, so there was no money to buy new clothes that fit.

I gave up. I bought some jeans and large shirts. I practically lived inside an oversized ankle-length black coat I found at a thrift store. I watched as people changed their attitudes toward me just because my appearance changed. I listened to the snickering comments and the snide remarks boys make to impress one another at the expense of whoever doesn't measure up to the standard of external beauty worshiped by our society. I stopped trying to look my best and began to console myself with food. What did it matter?

It was during this time that I became a Christian and began to hope that God would do a miracle to turn me back into the girl I used to be. I prayed and pleaded with God to free me from this terrible curse, but nothing seemed to happen. Finally, I decided to make the best of life as a fat girl.

I became active in drama, where my personality could shine even if I was always cast in character roles rather than the role of leading lady as I had once hoped. In one play I was cast as a middle-aged Jewish mother in a Woody Allen comedy. There was one scene where I was supposed to help another actor (playing the part of a slightly deranged priest) get untangled from a straitjacket. We were scripted to tangle up together and end up rolling about on the floor as my robe came undone, revealing a long-line girdle and undershirt. The scene ends with us flailing about on the floor and my wig falling off as someone enters the room. This scene was one of my favorites. Given my weight, I had no other opportunity for close physical contact with the opposite sex.

We were scheduled to videotape the dress rehearsal so we could review it before opening night. Dress rehearsal brings many new elements to the performance, not the least of which is dealing with costume changes and props. Somehow, in the excitement and confusion of my first dress rehearsal of my first real play, I forgot to put on the girdle and undershirt beneath my robe for this scene. I had on just my bra and panties. No one knew this until the moment when my robe fell open (with the video camera rolling). Everyone watching was horrified. It wasn't until after the scene was over that I realized I wasn't clothed properly. I was sure I would die. My life was over. I couldn't bear the thought that all my friends and classmates had seen me, that I couldn't remain hidden.

The thought of having to view the videotape, or of anyone else viewing it, was more than I could handle. I prayed harder than I had ever prayed before. The teacher told me that he planned to skip over that scene, so I was convinced it was okay to come back to class. But for some unexplained reason, the tape malfunctioned and none of the rehearsal was recorded. The class experienced a mixture of relief and frustration. They wanted to see the rehearsal, but no one wanted to come that close to seeing someone's worst fear realized. I like to think God intervened to cover my shame.

Even while I tried to hide, I also tried to hold on to the memory of the beauty I once saw in myself. The best way I found to cope was to drop out of the beauty race completely. I never wore makeup, I left my hair long but did nothing with it, and always wore the standard jeans and shirts. It was hard to keep trying when there seemed to be no hope of reward. I fell in love for the first time, like most girls do during high school, but I did my best not to betray my true feelings. I was just a good friend, a pal, one of the guys ... well, almost.

The boy I was infatuated with telephoned often to talk for long hours into the night. But at school he would rarely be seen with me. His girlfriend was a cheerleader whose locker was next to mine in gym class. She was beautiful, and I remember trying hard not to compare myself with her. On one level there was no comparison. But something inside me cried out against accepting that she was better than me or more worthy of someone's love just because she wore a size six and I didn't.

About this time, a woman at our church who was an actress and model offered a class for teenage girls on inner and outer beauty. I thought maybe it was worth taking the chance. The six-week class cost forty dollars each week. That was every penny I made at my after-school job, but I was desperate to find something of beauty within me. The class prompted me to try to make the best of my appearance, so I gathered up my courage and decided to see what kind of impression I could make (especially on a particular boy) if I put my best foot forward. I finished the class and saved enough money to buy a dress, stockings, and new high heels. I curled my long blond hair, applied makeup, painted my nails, put on the dress and stockings, and walked to school.

The first two classes of the day brought much encouragement. People were surprised to see me dressed up, but the compliments were plentiful. I had many friends, all of whom were happy to see me taking some care of my appearance. Third period was the moment of truth as far as I was concerned; *he* was in that class. My heart felt like it was in my throat as I walked into the classroom. Time seemed to stand still as he turned around, looked at me, and then began to laugh. "Hey, who are you trying to fool?" he said.

No one else in the class was laughing. It was all too obvious that I was devastated by his reaction. I turned around, walked the three miles home in my stocking feet. It didn't matter that I had ruined my hose. Nothing seemed to matter. Nothing I tried could make me beautiful. I received his verdict on my appearance as though it were the truth. When I got home, I threw the dress in the corner of my closet, changed back into my jeans, and washed the makeup off my face. I had tried to look my best, and I couldn't compete. It would be many years before I dared to wear a dress again.

I decided it was better not to try. I got up to 170 pounds before I left high school. I became depressed, spending much of my spare time plopped down on the couch, consoling myself with food. I believed God loved me, but I had stopped believing in my own beauty. Instead, I concentrated on developing my intellect and my spirit. I began taking college classes during my senior year, studied the Bible seriously, and took refuge in my growing knowledge of God. I was chosen salutatorian for our graduating class.

Through a rather miraculous turn of events (which I described in chapter two), I received a scholarship and grants to attend Pepperdine University in Malibu. I prepared to leave for college, still carrying a flame for the boy who laughed at my vain attempt to become beautiful.

• • •

PEPPERDINE'S MALIBU CAMPUS is situated in one of the most picturesque locations in California. Nestled on a hilltop, overlooking the ocean, it has a spectacular view of ocean sunsets, shimmering seas, and the ever-changing play of clouds over water. Behind the campus, the Santa Monica mountains have a beauty all their own. It's no wonder that celebrities who could afford to live anywhere choose to live just down the hill from Pepperdine, even though that means weathering earthquakes, mud slides, and wildfire. The beauty makes Malibu worth all the risks.

God had taken me from a junkyard to live in a brand-new dormitory on one of America's most beautiful campuses. I still didn't have much money for clothes. I couldn't hope to compete with the girls in my dorm, whose parents could afford to send them to school here. I had given up trying to improve my appearance. Instead, I began to focus on getting healthier. I started going to a nutritionist, ate only healthy foods, and discovered that I had a thyroid imbalance, which was treated successfully with medication. During this time I met Patrick. He accepted me as I was and always seemed to know there was more to me (or less when it came to my weight) than was on the surface.

My third year at Pepperdine I couldn't afford to live on campus so I responded to several ads that offered room and board in exchange for services. Several of the situations were less than desirable. I began to worry that I would be living in conditions reminiscent of home. I prayed, "Lord, please give me a place to live that will build me up, not tear down the sense of self-worth beginning to grow in me." His answer held far greater significance than I expected; it was a symbolic demonstration of how God was at work developing the beauty within me.

When I was growing up, several role models were held up as beautiful. The most familiar was Carol Merrill, the model on the game show "Let's Make A Deal." Carol Merrill was the Vanna White of her day. Our family always watched "the lovely Carol Merrill" revealing what was behind the curtain, the box, or doors number one, two, and three. She was beautiful and graceful, wore gorgeous clothes, and seemed to have a sparkling personality. From as early as I can remember, my dad had a crush on Carol Merrill.

Just as I was beginning to worry about finding a suitable place to live, an acquaintance mentioned that a woman named Carol needed an au pair to watch her daughter after school and help with light housekeeping in exchange for room and board. This woman turned out to be Carol Merrill, and I ended up living behind Door Number Three. Carol, her daughter Hillary, and I would make up a household where I could learn about order, self-care, beauty, and grace—all those things I had missed while growing up.

"Au pair" is a French phrase that means "to be on par with the rest of the family." Although I was working for my keep, I was always treated with respect, as a friend and an equal. My room was papered in white wallpaper with tiny flowers. The beam ceiling was sparkling white. The cabinets were also white, with a picture window that granted me a view of meadows tapering down to the ocean. The blond wood of the floors shone with my reflection when I walked across it. The antique lamp with its Tiffany stained glass and beaded fringe cast delicate colors against the walls. The oak frame for the full length mirror and the antique oak vanity were lovely in every detail. The white brass bed was made up with crisp, white linens, embroidered with shimmering white thread. Carol had no idea how much it meant to me at that time in my life to have such a beautiful room. But God knew the effect it would have for me to live in such surroundings and learn to be at home there.

Carol showed me how she liked to keep her home beautiful. She worked beside me, showing me how to clean and how to keep a schedule that kept the house looking its best. She enjoyed doing things to keep herself healthy and her home in order. She was kind, honest, and generous.

I watched Carol as she taught her daughter, who was twelve at the time, how to take care of herself. She never knew how much I appreciated being able to overhear the instruction of a mother to her daughter at this stage of development. When I was twelve, my mother was fighting her own battle with alcoholism, and my stepmother was struggling to keep ahead of my dad's mess-making. God knew. He took care to let me learn the things I needed to know in a beautiful way from a woman I respected, and who respected me in return.

While I lived at Carol's, I continued to eat healthfully and take better care of myself. When I needed formal attire for special events, Carol let me use selections from her wardrobe. Patrick proposed to me in Carol's beautifully decorated living room, before a romantic fire. Carol gave me a bridal shower, and Hillary greeted our guests at the top of the drive riding her horse, which she draped with a white sheet. At Christmas, Carol and Hillary gave me a delicate gold bracelet, more lovely than any I had ever owned.

In every way, Carol treated me as though I belonged in such a place, not as a servant, but as a person of great worth. She saw beyond my appearance to who I was and could be. When Pat and I married, we rented Carol's guest house for our first home. Shortly after we married, I lost all my extra weight and haven't had to struggle with it since. Through these people and situations, God helped me forget my past and dare to believe that the king desired my beauty.

It's been fifteen years since I lived with Carol and Hillary in Malibu. Although I still believe God desires my beauty, I still must resist the pull of the past. For years I felt out of place browsing in nice clothing stores or wearing makeup and dressing well. When I dress and groom myself to look my best, I experience an occasional twinge of fear that someone will look up and laugh and ask me, "Who are you trying to fool?" But I am growing to see that there was beauty within me all along. I just had to nurture it and bring it out by taking care of myself.

BELIEVING THAT GOD CREATED the beauty within each of us and wants it to come out is an exercise of faith. When you dare to believe in and express your own beauty, regardless of your past, your surroundings, or your appearance, taking care of yourself becomes fun.

Treating yourself well means believing in your own beauty and living as though your beauty is apparent to all. In the musical *My Fair Lady*, Eliza Doolittle explains to a confused Professor Higgins, "The difference between a flower girl and a lady is not in how she behaves, but in how she is treated." Treat yourself like the lady you are by filling your life with beauty. Read uplifting, well-written books; listen to the music you love; surround yourself with beautiful art and the wonders of nature. Soon you will realize that this is where you belong, and the beauty that has been hidden within you all along will blossom in its new, nurturing environment.

Beauty is often expressed through talents such as music, art, dance, interior decorating, writing, or other forms of creative expression. Begin to express your talents creatively where you are today in whatever ways you can. You may be surprised at the beauty you bring to your surroundings.

Whenever you share yourself genuinely, the beauty of your spirit will shine through even though you may not see it the way others do. When I speak at women's retreats, I often hear the comment, "Thank you for sharing your beautiful story." That strikes me as strange, because my story seems something other than beautiful to me. Living in the midst of the story, we tend to focus on the dirt in the garden of our lives rather than on the emerging blossoms. As I share myself with other women, I come to see through their response the beauty I would otherwise overlook.

Though you should be wary of expecting too much too soon, if you fail to take the first step because it seems so small, or because you feel so far behind where you think you should be, you'll never bring out your beauty. One step in the right direction will lead to the next.

An example of one small step leading to another is the battle I've fought with exercise ever since I became overweight during high school. I almost didn't graduate from college because I failed eight different physical education classes. It wasn't that I couldn't perform the exercises; I just always found some excuse to miss class. I hated comparing myself to others who seemed more capable. As a result, I wasted a lot of money, and I became less and less capable of being physically fit. But there has always been that little voice inside telling me life could be so much better if only I would exercise on a regular basis. Did I listen to that little voice? Sometimes. Did I actually start exercising? No. Did my body start to fall apart? Yes!

After giving birth to my third child, and while working on a lengthy writing assignment, my back went out. I went to the chiropractor, who dutifully put my back in place and urged me to exercise. My back went out again, and I worked for months lying flat on my back with the keyboard on a pillow over my legs. I went back to the chiropractor. He put my back in place and urged me to exercise. After we had repeated this sequence several times, and I had endured enough pain, I came up with this great idea. Hey, maybe I should start an exercise program!

So I made a decision to take a step in that direction. I didn't want to go to a class, I wanted something easy I could do in the privacy of my own home. I set out to sample exercise videos. I knew I couldn't bear to look at supermodels without hating them and ruining my spiritual life for hours, so I skipped those without a second look. I tried a program for more mature women that didn't work for me. I tried one for overweight women, but that just brought back bad memories and didn't take my aspirations in the right direction. Then I saw one taught by Barbie, the doll. I thought, "Hey, I can do this with Casey. Surely I can keep up with a twelve-inch doll." I found myself hating Barbie. Well, maybe it wasn't Barbie I hated. I hated the fact that at thirty-five years old, I was so void of physical stamina that I couldn't keep up with a plastic toy. Now I was in a quandary. I prayed, "Lord, you've got to help me. I'm further gone than I realized."

Shortly thereafter, I was browsing in the Sesame Street store while my kids played when I caught sight of a wonderful thing: "The Sesame Street Dance-Along Video." I bought it. When I played it the first time I knew I'd found the starting point for my exercise program. The Porker Sisters (three puppet pigs) were doing the pig shuffle. It's a simple little dance. You walk around the room singing, "I've got a new way to walk, walk, walk!" I looked great compared to the Porker Sisters. My kids and I had a fun time. We did "The Batty-Bat" with the Count and "The Pigeon" with Bert.

This was a tiny, baby step; but it was a step in the right direction. I later worked my way up to doing a real exercise video, designed as a first step for those just starting a physical fitness program. I slacked off for a while and my back went out again. But I started over and bought a cross-country ski machine. I started with the goal of using it two minutes a day, then five minutes, then ten minutes. It took a month or so, but I worked up to using it for twenty minutes. Compared to someone else, this progress may seem small. But I am not comparing myself to anyone else. I'm taking the steps I need to take to bring out the physical health and beauty that I trust is within me. However minuscule, the progress is there, and that counts for a great deal.

No matter where you are or how far you have to go, start where you are and take one step in the right direction. When you take care of yourself, your hidden beauty will spring up in due season.

Just as the prince saw the beauty in Cinderella and wanted to help her bring it out for all to see, God desires your beauty. He wants nothing more than to surround you with the sunshine, the rain, and the nutrients you need to cause the beauty within you to blossom.

NINE

Glass Slippers and Other Lost Treasures

Losing the remnants of your dreams and finding God's dreams for you

THE MOMENT CINDERELLA LOST her glass slipper, she had to make a choice: She could try to retrieve it or leave it behind and keep moving on. This beautiful, fragile slipper was part of her dream come true. It must have been difficult to let it go, even though Cinderella knew it would probably disappear at any second anyway. Perhaps she felt an instant of regret, a momentary compulsion to grasp this remnant of her dreams and try to hold on as long as she could.

Cinderella accepted the loss of her glass slipper and moved on. Ironically, her release of this remnant of her dreams became the means by which the prince could find her and give her the dreams he had planned for her. Her decision to let go of the slipper became the key to a future life that went far beyond her dream of attending the ball.

Oh, how beautiful and fragile are the dreams we dream for our lives! When we come close to having them come true, only to see them slip from our grasp, we too face a moment of decision. It is painfully difficult to accept this sort of loss and keep moving on with your life, especially when you believe the remnants of your dreams are the best your future may hold. However, when you remember that God has a future and a hope for you, that the God who loves you "is able to do immeasurably more than all we ask or imagine, according to his power that is at work within us" (Ephesians 3:20), then you will find the courage to let go when necessary.

Letting go of the remnants of lost dreams takes tremendous courage. If your dreams are dear to you, as they surely are, you want to protect them. You know they may be shattered if they are not held firmly in your grasp. And yet the mystery of life is this: Letting go, trusting the dreams you had for your life into the care of God, makes it possible for you to receive the dreams God has for you to become the woman of his dreams.

As the prince's servants charged out the palace gates, looking for the beautiful maiden, they took no notice of Cinderella sitting at the side of the road with her busted pumpkin, scurrying mice, and other pets. To them she was a nobody. But nearby, on the stairway of the palace, the Prince held her glass slipper near his heart as he said, "I must find her. I must have her. I won't be satisfied until she is my bride."

When we leave our losses behind, we may assume they are shattered and lost forever. But God himself picks up our lost treasures and holds them dear to his heart. He is respectful of their beauty and fragility. Others may look at us and see a nobody, especially in times of great loss. But we need not despair. If people have deemed you a nobody, remember, the prince has your lost treasures and is determined to find you. He won't give up until you are his and he can restore what you have lost. Then people will see who you really are. This knowledge gives you reason to smile, even though much may seem lost forever.

WHEN WE MOVED to northern California from Los Angeles, we started thinking about the possibility of buying a home. I had never given the matter a second thought when we lived in L.A. because real estate prices were so high and our youth ministry salary so low. However, in our new community, housing prices were so reasonable that most families, even those on modest incomes, were able to afford their own home. The dream of owning a home began to take root in my heart and mind.

When we faced our marriage crisis with a counselor, it became clear that Pat very much wanted our marriage to be restored and so did I. We started to dismantle the unsound parts of our old life and reconstruct a new one. As part of this process, the counselor suggested it might be helpful for us to affirm our commitment to building a life together by purchasing a home for our family. Besides, with a second baby on the way, we would need another bedroom.

To me, buying a house was as much symbolic of our hope for a good future together as it was practical. We found a comfortable little house: three bedrooms, one bath, living room and kitchen— in all, 830 square feet of living space. It had an attached garage, covered patio, and a small fenced backyard where the kids could play. We bought it from the original owner, a widow who had lived there fourteen years and kept the house immaculate. Her asking price: $57,000. We closed escrow December 18.

That January (less than one month later) we told the pastor about Pat's fall and found ourselves both unemployed. Now we had a house, but no way to make even the modest mortgage payments. However, the house had become the symbol of our new life together, and I wasn't about to let go without a fight. We borrowed and prayed and scraped together whatever we could to get through those first few months. Working on the house became a kind of therapy all its own. Painting and decorating Casey's room and the nursery for the new baby kept us sane during the months when Pat could not find work and I couldn't bear idle hours. Then Pat found a job that helped pay the mortgage. When Taylor was born in May, we took solace in the home God knew we would need so greatly during this season of our lives.

Month by month, over the course of a year, it became apparent that there was no future for us in that town, but I couldn't bear to lose the only home we had ever owned. Each room bore the imprint of our love for each other and our children, the love that brought color back into our lives when our family was threatened. How could I let it go?

Finally, Pat sat down with me and convinced me that if we didn't choose to move to another city where he could find a better career, we would lose the house by foreclosure. Reason won out in my mind, even while my heart was breaking. I would take Casey to kindergarten, then come home and sit in her room, crying. We had made it so beautiful for her: the careful stenciling, the wallpaper that wasn't allowed in a rental. Every detail of our decorating made me cry at the thought of moving.

I told God I didn't know how I could possibly move away. I thought that if I gave up this house I might never get another one. It was hard enough to give up my career and ministry. I didn't know if I could bear the loss of my home as well.

My options quickly came down to these: I could insist on staying and risk losing the house, agree to move without giving the house over to God (and deal with the resentment that surely would weigh me down), or let go and give my treasured dreams of having a home over to the care of God. I had walked with God long enough to know that the best option by far was the last. We rented the house out and moved back to southern California, where Pat took a better job. We found a nice two-bedroom apartment a few miles from our counselor's office. There we took advantage of the counseling freely offered us, and I started grieving for all I had lost. In the course of time I was able to let go more, and we sold the house for a profit (which we needed to help offset the debts we had incurred while trying to hold on to it).

Within six months of our move to southern California, the opportunity arose for me to write devotionals. My grief and experiences with turning my life over to the care of God became a wealth of raw material I used to help others who were hurting and trying to recover. It was an opportunity I would never have been given if I had insisted on staying in northern California.

After eighteen months in southern California our counseling was complete, and Pat transferred to a position with his company in the Sacramento area. We thought this might be a nice place to settle down and raise our family, and housing prices were reasonable enough to rekindle our dreams of buying a home.

We had two years in which to reinvest the money (now long gone) from the sale of the first house or pay capital gains taxes. According to our accountant, the taxes would be equal to the amount of a down payment and closing costs for another house. I left the matter in God's hands, but reminded him of my prayer that he restore what we had lost. It seemed obvious that it would be better to buy another house rather than just give the money to the Internal Revenue Service, but we had ruined our good credit rating while we were out of work and without income. Getting the money together before the two year deadline seemed impossible in itself, and even if we could raise the money, we had much work to do to repair our credit record.

We decided to do our best to try to buy a house before the deadline of April 9, 1994. We worked as hard as we could to earn and save the money, worked with our creditors to pay off as many bills as we could, and attempted to clear our credit record of as many negative marks as possible. As 1993 drew to a close, we saw no way to qualify for a loan, even if we could come up with the money for a down payment and closing costs. We prayed about it and occasionally looked at homes in our area when we saw an open house sign. Once we even dared to apply for a mortgage loan. When we were turned down, we decided not to torment ourselves by looking at any more houses.

Then the kids and I saw a house for sale by owner that we couldn't resist looking at. It was beautifully decorated, affordably priced, and had a great yard. The kids fell in love with the house and the yard, especially because it had a duck pond complete with a duck. "Oh, Mommy, can we buy this house?" they begged. I began to wish I had never brought them in to get their hopes up. But I also found myself wishing the house could be ours, wishing it had four bedrooms instead of three, and dreaming of who would have which bedroom—all those things real estate sales people want prospective home buyers to start dreaming. But I knew we couldn't really buy the house, so I dragged my kids away from the duck and headed home to our rented house.

A few days later the owner of the home called me, asking if we were interested. I told him we were, but that we couldn't qual-ify for a loan at the present time. He was highly motivated to sell right away and asked me to let his lender run the figures and see if we could qualify. How could I turn down this desperate man? Besides, what could it hurt to try again? This time the lender found a way to qualify us for the loan. Now I had to tell the seller we had no money for a down payment or closing costs. But hope began to swell within me. Maybe God would come through and let us have this beautiful house that was far better than the one we sold. It seemed a miracle that we had even qualified for the loan. Why would it be so hard for God to give me another writing project or some other unexpected source of funds?

So Pat and I went to the house together. When I looked it over again, I loved it more than at first. We began to let our hearts treasure the dream of owning this home. When we couldn't come up with the money, we tried to negotiate a lease with an option to buy. My heart was set on having this home, and with God's help I was determined to find a way.

But another buyer came along with cash in hand, and we lost the house.

Whenever you allow your heart to hope for something and you lose it, you must grieve it. So I hashed out my feelings with God in prayer, trying to understand why he would let me hope again only to be disappointed. Then it dawned on me that something good had come from this sequence of events: We now knew that we could qualify for a loan of a certain amount. So we were encouraged to look for houses in that price range. Unfortunately, we saw nothing in our price range that compared to the house we had lost out on.

As Pat and I prayed together, the Holy Spirit seemed to say, "What do you really want? What does your family need?" What we needed and wanted was a four-bedroom house. It seemed ridiculous to even think of a four-bedroom home when we couldn't find a three-bedroom that we could afford, but this was not the first time God had encouraged us to lay the true desires of our heart before him in prayer. So we confessed secretly to God that, yes, we did want a four-bedroom house.

By the beginning of November we had a clear vision of what our family needed, and we were clearly convinced that there was no way we could make this happen. Finally, after we had done all we could do, we prayed a prayer of relinquishment. "Dear Father, we give up. We've done all we can do. We are not giving up in despair. At least we know we tried our best, but we are giving the whole issue of getting another house over to you. If we don't get a house by April 9, please help us come up with the tax money. If we do get a house, by some miracle (since we still don't have any money for a down payment and closing costs), we will give you all the credit. Amen!"

Within a few days I received a call from my literary agent. He had a project that needed to be done in six weeks for a substantial amount of money, enough to reduce our debts and cover the money we needed up front to buy a house. I jumped at the chance.

Pat and I set out in our car to start looking for houses—quickly. We drove by a house we had admired every time we went for our regular walk, a nearly new tri-level, four-bedroom home, with over 2,000 square feet of living space. This day the sign out front noted a considerable drop in price. We were the first interested parties to call the agent after the seller decided to drop his asking price to a price sure to sell. It was ten thousand dollars more than what we previously qualified for, but Pat had received a raise at work that week so we thought we might be able to qualify for the higher amount. The realtor called a lender he trusted (a man who seemed able to work miracles on his own), and within a few weeks God gave us our home. We moved in April 1, one week before our tax deadline.

There are several lessons I draw from this experience:

- From the moment we gave the whole matter over to God and let go, a power far greater than the full force of our human abilities went to work behind the scenes to answer our prayers. People, timing of events, and circumstances were moved into place for our benefit.

- God led us to a home far better than either of the ones I would have settled for if I could have forced the circumstances to cooperate with my plans. When we let go of the remnants of our lost dreams, we opened up the possibility for God to give us the dreams he had for us. These dreams satisfied the deepest desires of our hearts and were far better than we would have dared imagine. The Bible says that as high as the heavens are above the earth, so high are God's ways compared to our human ways. Is it any wonder that when we trust God to fulfill our deepest desires and dreams his way, the result is better than doing it our way?

- The process for finding God's best for us was treasuring our dreams and aspirations, losing those treasured dreams, and then surrendering the treasures of our heart to God. This process tests and purifies our faith. It also displays the glory of God in a way others can see tangibly.

- All things, the gains and the losses, were woven together by God into a tapestry. During times of loss we felt tremendous pain, but we also saw the grace of God woven into our lives. We held on to hope in God's promise to cause all things to work together for good to us because we love him and are called according to his purpose.

- The process was stressful and hard to bear as long as I was clutching at my dreams and trying to fight off God and everyone else who I thought wanted to rob me of that which I held dear. Once I let go and admitted that apart from God I could do nothing, the process became much less worrisome. Learning to trust your lost treasures to the care of God can eliminate a great source of stress.

When I say "let go and let God," or entrust your life and losses to the care of God, I say it within the context of an active, ongoing commitment to do your best to fulfill your responsibilities as well. God has given us resources, creative power, free will, raw talent, and abilities, and he expects us to use these to fulfill our roles and commitments in life. We are to do the very best we can to use every talent and resource God puts at our disposal. When we do the best we can with what we have, then we can confidently let go and let God do his part.

If we are doing our best and things aren't working out the way we want them to, that is when we need to let go. Do the best you can, pray that it is blessed, and then leave the rest in God's hands. It may help to practice the Serenity Prayer: "God, grant me the serenity to accept the things I cannot change, the courage to change the things I can, and the wisdom to know the difference. Amen."

Letting go and letting God take over does not mean disconnecting our emotions; it is important to grieve what we have lost. We can be assured that God is with us even through tremendous pain. Some people, in fact, sense God's presence more keenly when they are grieving than at any other time. David wrote in the Psalms that God collected his tears in a bottle. After going through times of loss, I grew to trust that God shared my pain and knew every teardrop.

Everyone will experience losses in the course of life. Each person must choose whether to keep their hearts turned toward God during these times or turn away. The pain of those who turn away from God is wasted; it merely drives them to despair or cynicism. But for those who entrust their losses to God, the pain and loss become a key to discovering new depths of his mercy and compassion.

Jeremiah was called the weeping prophet because he cried over Israel when she was taken over by the Babylonians. In the middle of his book of Lamentations, you find the key to what gave him hope: "This I call to mind and therefore I have hope: Because of the LORD's great love we are not consumed, for his compassions never fail. They are new every morning; great is your faithfulness. I say to myself, 'The LORD is my portion; therefore I will wait for him.' The LORD is good to those whose hope is in him, to the one who seeks him; it is good to wait quietly for the salvation of the LORD" (Lamentations 3:21–26).

The ability to let go and let God take care of our lives creates an atmosphere in which we can receive back the very thing we desire, but with peaceful assurance, not fearful desperation. In the course of life, God may use our losses and potential losses to test our trust in him and our willingness to let go. One of the classic ways God tests us is to ask us to give up the very things and people he has given us. Genesis records the story of how Abraham waited more than fourteen years for God to fulfill his specific promise that a son would be born to him. Isaac was born long after Abraham or his wife should have been physically able to conceive a child. He was to be the one to bless future generations of Israel and, through Israel, the whole world. We can only imagine Abraham's horror when God asked him to surrender on an altar of sacrifice the very son God miraculously gave him.

Hebrews 11:17–19 tells us that, "By faith Abraham, when God tested him, offered Isaac as a sacrifice. He who had received the promises was about to sacrifice his one and only son, even though God had said to him, 'It is through Isaac that your offspring will be reckoned.' Abraham reasoned that God could raise the dead, and figuratively speaking, he did receive Isaac back from death." Abraham had prepared the altar, laid out his son on it, and raised his knife for the kill when the angel of God stopped his hand and showed him a ram caught by its horns in a bush. God had provided his own substitute for the sacrifice of Abraham's son. Abraham named that spot "The LORD Will Provide," because that was where he learned that by being willing to obey God without reservation, God miraculously provided what was needed.

Only when Abraham was willing to let go of his dream—his treasured child—did he receive from the angel the reassurance of the Lord's promise to bless Abraham's descendents. Abraham had to let go completely, trusting that God would take care of him and keep his promises no matter what.

I have seen this paradox in my own life. When I gave up my hopes of love with the young man I set my heart on during high school, God brought me a husband who proved to be a far better match. I saw Patrick as the answer to many prayers, my reward for trusting God with the loss of the earlier relationship. Then came the day my marriage was in peril, and I was faced with the very real possibility that I might lose this relationship as well. I wanted my marriage to survive this crisis, but I also realized my heart could go one of two ways. I could clutch at the relationship and try to force it to work by desperately clinging to Pat and by checking up on his every move, or I could entrust the relationship to the care of God.

During the season when our marriage could have gone either way, my willingness to let go and let God take care of me helped our marriage survive. I acknowledged that Pat could very well turn away from his commitment, as could I. I stopped trying to manipulate him into making me feel safe again in the relationship. I stopped trying to force anything. Instead, I nestled into God. In my mind, I put my marriage on the altar and said, "If it's dead, it's dead." Even Jesus accepted the possibility of divorce in specific circumstances. Facing the reality of this was like preparing to sacrifice that which I held most dear, but I was able to say, "I still know God will take care of me as long as I keep trusting him. God is God. He has the power to stop the unraveling of this relationship and resurrect our marriage. Either way, I am going to continue to trust that God will take care of me and lead me to the destiny he has planned for me."

This attitude of trust in the face of possible loss, this stance of letting go and letting God take control, preceded a beautiful healing of our relationship. By counting our marriage and everything we had known in the past as loss, I allowed myself to press on to a better future.

Pat chose to put the past behind him as well, and recommited himself to me and to our sacred vows. Together, we faced the future with a renewed love and enthusiasm. By placing our lives and losses on the altar of surrender, we had affirmed our love for and trust in God. In turn, God had affirmed his love for us and his supreme power over our lives by giving us back what we surrendered.

• • •

SOON AFTER I accepted Christ, I sensed the call of God in my life. I wasn't sure what that meant, but my keen interest in the teenagers who showed up at our door hungry for God caused me to suppose that they were my life's calling. I eagerly pursued youth ministry and thought that would be my life's work. Just before we moved to northern California to begin what I thought was going to be the fulfillment of my life's dream, the church staff I was leaving spent time praying for me as a group, asking God's blessing and guidance for my life. While we prayed, a woman on staff named Johanna Molloy said she kept getting a mental picture as she prayed for me.

She described a scene where I stood in a large plowed field, wearing an apron with many pockets around the front. I reached into the pocket nearest my right hand and brought out a handful of seed of all one kind. I scattered the seed, and a crop sprang up where the seeds landed. Then I reached my hand back into that same pocket, again bringing out a handful of the same kind of seed as before. As I lifted my hand, beginning to scatter the seed again, a hand reached down from above and pried my fingers loose, forcing me to let go. Then the hand put my fingers into one of the other pockets I had previously neglected. Following his indications, I put both hands into the other pockets and brought out handfuls of all kinds of seeds. I scattered them, and this time the seeds went further and a larger crop sprang up, but the crop was a mixture of many kinds of plants.

I tend to be cautious whenever anyone offers spiritual insight that I am not sure is from God, but I politely listened as Johanna explained what she thought this mental image or vision meant. She said the first seed indicated my ministry to youth, the first handful being the ministry I had done at their church. The next handful represented my continuing ministry to youth. The mixed seed in the other pockets represented a ministry of broader appeal that would reach out to all ages and many groups of people. Johanna said it seemed the broader ministry would supersede my initial youth ministry. She didn't focus any attention on the part where my hand had to be pried loose from the original seed.

I thanked her and thought to myself at the time that she had a vivid imagination. I wanted no part of any other kind of ministry. My heart was set on working with teenagers. It was only later, after God had to literally wrench my grip loose from the ministry I loved, that I recalled Johanna's word picture with fresh interest. Surely God was preparing my mind and heart to understand that it was only when I let go of what I wanted that I could fill my hands with what God had for me. After I did let go and began writing, I found a great sense of peace and fulfillment.

SOME PEOPLE SAY that things work out for the best in time. I don't believe this is always true. Letting go is not enough—we must let go *and* turn our lives over to the care of God. In the course of nature, things don't get better when left to work out on their own. The law of the universe shows us that when left to themselves, things go from good to bad and from bad to worse, from order to disorder, from growth to decay. If we cast our cares to the wind, they will only be blown away. But if we cast all our cares upon God, he will make things work out for the best.

We will only dare to cast our cares upon God, however, if we have the assurance that he cares for us. We must believe God is there for us, and that he rewards those who diligently seek him, before we will look for opportunities to commit our losses and cares to him. We must learn to pray, asking God for what we need and waiting patiently for the Lord to provide for these needs on a daily basis.

Learning to let go of lost treasures and entrusting them to the care of God has many benefits. It will allow you to see life as an adventure in which you can enjoy whatever comes your way instead of seeing life as a game you must play perfectly in order to win. You will also be able to rest. It takes a great deal of energy to try to play God. When you learn to let God be God, you can relax and simply enjoy worshiping him. By counting everything as loss, and having nothing left to lose, you are given the freedom to be real, to be imperfect. And by trusting God to take care of your reputation, you won't have to try to control the way other people perceive you. You will be able to use all of your life, even the parts you used to be ashamed of, to encourage others who struggle with the kinds of losses you have survived.

While talking about this subject with my daughter Casey, she asked what benefit could possibly come from the greatest loss she has known, the death of Granny Edith. In answering her question I realized there is hope to be found even in the most profound and lasting kind of loss. When we lose a loved one through death, the hope of eternal life and heaven gain greater appeal to our hearts. Jesus said that where our treasures are, there our hearts would be also. We are also encouraged to seek those things above, where Christ is seated at the right hand of the Father. Knowing that those we have loved and lost have preceded us into eternity draws our hearts heavenward.

Death was not part of God's original plan for humanity; it came as part of the curse from the fall. Even though death became a reality, I see the grace of God in the way he staggered our lives so that they would overlap. If we all lived and died at the same time, then we would miss out on our connection with the eternal while we were alive. But by allowing us to see the deaths of those who lived before us, God gives us hope in eternity. Because Jesus came, tasted death, and then demonstrated victory over death, we have hope in the face of the greatest loss of all. That which makes no sense from a temporal perspective will become clear in light of eternity and God's eternal purposes. This knowledge gives us the courage and faith to accept our losses, grieve them, and keep moving toward God's goal for us here and hereafter.

Abraham was promised the entire land of Israel as his inheritance, but during his life on earth the only property he actually held the deed to was the grave in which he buried Sarah and in which he himself was buried. However, his life demonstrated that he had learned to trust God's promise to him. The kingdom Abraham was looking for was the eternal kingdom of God, a kingdom not of this world, one in which there will be no more death or loss. By trusting God with our losses and drawing near to the One who holds our lost treasures near to his heart, we too can be assured that we will one day live forever in the eternal kingdom of God.

I SEE ONE LAST REASON that God may allow us to lose our treasures: Sometimes we don't realize the value of what we have. We may hide away something God wants us to share with the world. Sometimes the best way, maybe the only way, God is able to do all he dreams of doing with our lives is to take something we treasure out of our hands.

Margaret Fishback Powers wrote a poem that has become dear to millions. It is most commonly known as "Footprints." Perhaps you have read it on a plaque, a poster, or a coffee mug.

What you may not know is that Margaret, the author of the poem, lost a box containing her poetry during a move and only years later saw her poem when it was published anonymously. The poem touched such a resonant chord with people around the globe that it has become one of the most widely read and widely published pieces of contemporary poetry. Margaret spent many years in legal pursuits, trying to convince the publishers and others making money off of her work that she indeed was the author before her persistence finally paid off. Not only has she been acknowledged as the poem's author, but her story has become a book—*Footprints: The True Story Behind the Poem that Inspired Millions.*

God took Margaret's lost treasure and used it for great gain. Even though those who used her work without acknowledging her authorship were wrong, God eventually turned the situation around to work out right. We will never know if this poem would have had as great a reception if Margaret Powers had kept it in her control instead of losing it. What we *do* know is that God can use our losses to do something "immeasurably more than all we ask or imagine."

Perhaps God takes our treasures completely out of our hands at times in order to transform our character. Trusting God with our lost treasures tests us as nothing else does. When he returns our treasures to us at his appointed time, God not only sees our desires fulfilled, he sees our love for him deepened, our character refined, and our faith purified.

Our treasures may be lost to us, but they are never lost to God. Just as the prince used the lost slipper to find Cinderella and give her all the riches of his kingdom, God may use our losses to turn our hearts toward him. And in the process, he changes us into women who can enjoy the treasures of God's kingdom forever.

TEN

At The Stroke Of Midnight

Refusing to revert to your old rags

CINDERELLA'S DREAM CAME TRUE. She was splendidly beautiful for an evening. And yet, at the stroke of midnight, the magic dissipated. It only took a moment for her to dissolve into what she once was. She was left on a dirt road, clothed in tattered rags. All she had left to hold on to were a glass slipper and memories of how wonderful life had been dancing in the arms of the prince. These alone kept her hoping that he would not forget her.

When it comes to matters of the Spirit, what seems clear as crystal one moment may dissolve into doubts the next. You might be experiencing a closeness with God that is transforming your life—and your image of yourself—spiritually, emotionally, intellectually, and socially. Then, without warning, something happens that wipes away all the confidence you once had in God, as well as your confidence in your own beauty or personal worth. The good life God provided for you as you followed him becomes destroyed by a loss, a failure, a tragedy that strikes near to your heart, or any other circumstance that triggers old feelings and fears.

During times when the fulfillment of past promises has disappeared and you are left wondering if the rest of God's promises can possibly come true, it is the memories of dancing in the arms of God that will help you go on. The quality of your previous relationship with God will directly influence whether you will persevere in your belief that God will not forget you. Having danced in the arms of God will help you refuse to revert to your old rags when life gets rough.

My dreams all seemed to be coming true: I was working alongside Pat in youth ministry and enjoying a loving marriage and growing family. When all of that fell apart, my dream come true dissolved into a distorted nightmare. It seemed as though a villain stepped in and locked me into a hopeless situation. The nightmare that started August 12, 1988, when Pat confessed to me, dragged on for years with no sign of a happy ending, no visible signs of God's promises coming true.

This crisis was the greatest test of faith I have ever known, and it was made more difficult because no one in particular was watching to see how I fared. In the past, being a role model to the kids in the youth group had been an added motivation to obey God. But no one was watching anymore except God, and he seemed distant. Could I hold on to my faith? Could I wait quietly for God to come to my rescue? Could I continue to hope that I would ever make it to my dreams?

ON APRIL 5, 1989, three months after Pat and I lost our ministry positions, a visiting minister held a special service at our church to exercise his gift of prophecy. I was hesitant, and came only at the encouragement of our pastor. I hoped that if the man ministered a true gift of prophecy, he might tell the church leaders to reinstate me to my position.

The minister arrived late, so he had no opportunity to learn anything about our situation before the meeting began. I was relieved at this, because I thought the pastor might fill him in on our situation and then try to influence us through something this man might say in the name of God.

About seventy-five people had gathered in the room above the main auditorium. It was a room filled with both wonderful and painful memories for me. We had often used it for youth functions, and it was the place where we had last met with the kids immediately after Pat's confession. Today, the entire church staff was in the room, and I found that it hurt to sit with those I used to minister alongside when they had no intentions of welcoming me back. By the time we finished with worship, I was overcome with emotion and couldn't hold back the tears.

The minister paced the room, praying until he sensed a prophecy for a particular person. I was one of the first he approached. I was obviously upset. He held his hand out toward me and spoke.

"Be strengthened and encouraged for the hand of the Lord is truly upon you," he said. "And surely the Lord would say, 'Don't worry, for thou shalt see that even by the outpouring of my water and of my wine, and of my oil, I'm going to cause great changes to be.'

"I see the word coming to you in a very fresh way. It's going to bring refreshing in the midst of thee, and cause you to say, 'It's a fresh drink. It's like fresh melted snow. And I can sense within me the life of Christ as it does grow.'

"Also, he's going to pour forth the oil of his Spirit anointing within thee, afresh and anew. And you're going to rejoice in what his anointing shall truly do. But watch out for the wine, for he's going to give thee not just a drop, but he's going to pour it into thee in abundance until joy becomes the very fruit of his cup. And yea, great joy shall he restore in the midst of thee, as surely he sets your spirit free."

At this point I was still in tears. It was obvious I had no joy at that moment. At least I could be sure the minister wasn't making up something by reading my expression.

He continued, "Look about thee, at the shakings that have come, the devastation that would try to destroy that which the Lord has done, and yea, lift your eyes from that quickly and set them upon the Christ, which is truly thy choice. And watch and see. He's going to cause even that which will cause you to rejoice. I see some hurts, some scars, some bruises. Don't look at them anymore. Know that the Holy Spirit, by his oil, his wine, and his water, is removing them completely. And you'll find that that which was a bruise will become a stone to stand upon, a declaration that will help others as they move along. For God is faithful. He will not—" he raised his voice—"*he will not* allow you to be destroyed. But he's even increasing you, and yea, he's bringing you forth as a shining one. And yea, that which has been shaken around you shall shine forth, too."

The congregation broke into applause. The next day I listened to the tape of the prophecy and wrote it in my prayer journal. I decided to search the Scriptures for references to oil and wine to see how the terms were used figuratively in the Bible.

I found some applicable verses in the second chapter of Joel. The prophet Joel addressed the nation of Israel after they had seen swarms of locusts destroy their crops and their agricultural economy. Joel pronounced that this devastation on the whole nation was divine judgment for sin. *Surely,* I thought, *there must have been some who did not participate in the sin, but who suffered devastation along with those who did.*

I took comfort in the portion of Joel's prophecy that brought a message of hope to devastated people of God. He proclaimed that the Lord would "take pity on his people." The Lord would say to them: "I am sending you grain, new wine and oil, enough to satisfy you fully; never again will I make you an object of scorn to the nations" (Joel 2:19). Pat and I too had been the object of scorn. "I will repay you for the years the locusts have eaten....You will have plenty to eat, until you are full, and you will praise the name of the LORD your God, who has worked wonders for you; never again will my people be shamed." (Joel 2:25–26).

I took comfort in this last verse because we were almost down to our last dollar. The baby was due in a few weeks, and we weren't sure how we would be able to buy groceries. I took Joel's prophecy as encouragement that God would provide the food we needed.

By May 13 we had just sixty-one cents, with two weeks to wait until Pat's next paycheck. I went into labor and gave birth to Taylor the next day. Women from church brought us homemade dinners every night for the next two weeks. Each dear woman brought more than enough food to eat for dinner and throughout the next day, as well as love, encouragement, words of support, and gifts for Taylor and Casey. We had more than enough to eat until Pat's next paycheck.

For the next several years we figuratively wandered through the wilderness, but our shoes never got holes in them and our clothes never wore out. I eventually realized that there was no hope of my dreams for reinstatement coming true. I lapsed in and out of depression. The hope I had always had for our lives, hope that God would redeem our situation, came and went. I began to think God would use our lives, but maybe only to show people the ravages of sin. And yet I persevered in my faith.

People would sometimes ask me, "How can you continue to trust God and go to church after all that has happened?" I felt like the disciples must have felt when Jesus' tough message caused the crowds to turn away from following him: "'You do not want to leave too, do you?' Jesus asked the Twelve. Simon Peter answered him, 'Lord, to whom shall we go? You have the words of eternal life. We believe and know that you are the Holy One of God'" (John 6:67–69).

When I committed my life to Christ, I was convinced that Jesus was the express image of the invisible God. I didn't stay with him because I didn't feel like running away; I stayed because I couldn't escape my own beliefs. I knew he was true. I knew he loved me. I knew how much he had done for me over our years together.

God was as real to me as my husband. There is no one that could convince me Patrick Neal wasn't a real person. I lived with him. I had known his love over the course of many years. I could see the children he and I gave birth to through our love for one another. While there had been times Pat seemed distant from me, I had never doubted his existence or my commitment to him in marriage. The same was true of my relationship with God.

It had taken years of diligent Bible study, vigorous testing of every doubt, and the intellectual convictions of a reasoned faith to build up my confidence in the Word of God. Now came the test to see whether what had been established would uphold me securely. Or would my life, built on faith in God's Word, be swept away in a raging sea of doubt or difficulties?

• • •

IN 1977, WHEN I LIVED in Malibu, great storms threatened the beachfront homes in Malibu Colony. The Colony is an exclusive stretch of beach where the rich and famous live. When the storm threatened their homes, the people living in Malibu Colony called Pepperdine University with a cry for help. Hundreds of us were roused from sleep by the urgent announcement on the dorm intercom system. For five days and nights we toiled, filling sandbags, carrying them through incredibly lavish homes, and wrestling against the waves to keep some kind of foundation underneath so that the homes would not crash into the sea.

When the storms were over, a few of us walked down onto the beach, which was now thirty feet lower than it had been a week before. We looked back at the beleaguered mansions from a new perspective. The sight was staggering! From this vantage point we could see their precarious situation. These mansions had no foundation; they had literally been built on sand. Many of them were lost entirely, crumbled and splintered under the force of the waves, and then carried away to be tossed up on some other shore. Those that had not fallen were upheld by what appeared to be stilts, wooden beams that reached deep enough into the sand so the mansion didn't wash away. While these supports held them— barely—they certainly did not have the kind of firm foundation most people want to hold up everything they treasure in life.

Jesus taught that we need the firm foundation of hearing his Word and doing what he says in order to endure the storms of life. My own life had just been through a major storm. When I finally stepped back and looked at it from a distance, I could see that the reason my life and faith had not collapsed was that I had been building on that firm foundation of my spiritual life for many years.

For a little girl, it may be enough to sing "Jesus loves me, this I know for the Bible tells me so," but when we grow up to be women, we must, at some point, know *why* we believe the Bible and why we believe Jesus' teachings recorded in it. I continued to be faithful, not as an emotional response to a proposal of love from God, but because of my reasoned understanding of the teachings of Jesus.

The intellectual confidence I had in Jesus' teachings gave me a sturdy basis for reexamining my life. Cemented in the foundation of my life were promises God had fulfilled. Each one was like a precious stone, commemorating a time God had proved himself true to his word. Reminding myself of how God had previously instructed me, lead me, comforted me, and brought forth new life in those I loved, gave me hope that he would fulfill other promises as well.

While spending time with the Lord, the Holy Spirit would sometimes lead me to a verse of Scripture that seemed to be meant for me at just that moment. I would write these in my prayer journal. During the time when I was afraid our marriage might not survive, I found comfort in Isaiah 54 and 61. Although I knew these promises were originally written for the nation of Israel, the Spirit of God seemed to be saying, "Connie, these promises are for you."

When I found out about Pat's fall, it seemed as though the husband I knew had died. For a time, I felt as alone as a widow. All the reproach and shame we endured made me fear what the future might hold. But these verses from Isaiah comforted me: "'Do not be afraid; you will not suffer shame. Do not fear disgrace; you will not be humiliated. You will forget the shame of your youth and remember no more the reproach of your widowhood. For your Maker is your husband—the LORD Almighty is his name—the Holy One of Israel is your Redeemer; he is called the God of all the earth. The LORD will call you back as if you were a wife deserted and distressed in spirit—a wife who married young, only to be rejected,' says your God. 'For a brief moment I abandoned you, but with deep compassion I will bring you back'" (Isaiah 54:4–7).

I was extremely concerned about my own children. I worried that the trauma of the situation might endanger the baby while I was carrying it. I was also distraught that the kids in the youth group, whom I thought of as my own, would be destroyed emotionally and spiritually by the disappointment of my husband's fall and the way the church was mishandling it. To these worries God offered this promise: "All your sons will be taught by the LORD, and great will be your children's peace" (Isaiah 54:13).

Yet another promise that meant much to me was Isaiah 61:7: "Instead of their shame my people will receive a double portion, and instead of disgrace they will rejoice in their inheritance; and so they will inherit a double portion in their land, and everlasting joy will be theirs." I didn't tell anyone that I knew God was going to give me back double for all my shame—I could hardly believe it myself at the time. But as I took comfort in these promises and prayed that God might apply them to my life, my hope grew a little stronger every day.

I RECALLED THAT along with all the good promises, God also promised trouble, and Jesus promised his followers that they would face rejection in this world. Those aren't the kinds of promises we want to hear, but when troubles come, we shouldn't be taken by surprise.

I remember talking to a friend from high school who I had not seen for many years. I had introduced him to Jesus when we were both in tenth grade. When we met again, more than a decade later, he was going through a bitter divorce. "I wish someone would have told me how hard life was going to be," he said. "Now I look back in the Bible, and I see the warnings were there. But people only told me the happy promises, the God-will-give-you-what-you-want promises. I think I would have been better off if they had presented the good with the bad up front. I wish someone had let me know God promised never to leave me in the midst of the pain."

My friend had a good point. Jesus did say he came to give us abundant life, but he also said, "I have told you these things, so that in me you may have peace. In this world you will have trouble. But take heart! I have overcome the world" (John 16:33).

I determined not to turn my back on God just because I was facing a difficult season of life. If this promise of trouble was true—Jesus certainly seemed sure about it—it didn't diminish my faith in his other promises; in fact, it actually reinforced my faith. I had decided to follow Jesus. There was no turning back.

While my commitment remained firm, my emotions were raging. The wonderful plan I thought God had for my life had fallen apart, and it was left to me to grapple with how to make sense of it all. I wondered at God's undisclosed reasons for allowing me to know such deeply disturbing pain. I cried out to him, "So this is it? This is the wonderful plan you have for my life? Well, it's not wonderful! It's hardly bearable! If you love me and have a wonderful plan for my life, could you please enlighten me, because I don't see it!"

Have you ever been to a suspense film with someone who has already seen it? If you have, you know that during those scenes when the heroine is in danger and the tension is almost unbearable, you can glance at your companion to see if you need to worry. Your tension will be relieved if that person calmly smiles or tells you it will be okay. Then, instead of worrying that the heroine will be destroyed, your mind is free to wonder about how she will get out of her predicament.

When Cinderella's dreams dissolve in the dust, there is no need to worry because you know the end of the story. You know that her difficult circumstances are the pathway to a great future. I could only hope there was some truth to the parallels I saw between the Cinderella story and the kind of life I thought the Bible promised me.

When I saw no way to rise above my circumstances and reach the happy ending I had hoped for—after I prayed my "So-this-is-the-wonderful-plan-you-have-for-my-life?" prayer—I became aware of God's presence. I sensed him beside me, watching this scene of my life, and when I noticed him there, he calmly smiled. He already knew why my life was taking these unexpected twists. He assured me that I could relax and keep watching. He did indeed have a wonderful plan for my life, a plan that would unfold as I stayed close to him.

This new perspective helped me change my attitude. I said to God, "Smile if you like! Show me how you plan to get me out of this mess. You said you have plans for me, for good and not for evil, to give me a future and a hope. Well, I've lost sight of the future I had in mind, but I'm not going to give up now. If I did, I would never know what you might have done to turn this situation around for good in my life. This I've got to see!"

God will comfort our hearts with promises. We cannot assume every promise made to others in the Bible automatically applies to us, but God can apply any of his promises to us if he so chooses. If you find yourself attracted to a Scripture promise that you are not sure applies to your situation, write it in your promise notebook or prayer journal along with the date and what you think the promise might mean for your life. Then ask the Holy Spirit to reveal if this promise is truly for you and ask God for understanding. If the promise doesn't come to pass the way you thought God intended, nothing is lost. If God confirms it, then tell the world. By paying attention to the prompting of the Holy Spirit and by keeping track of these promises, it is possible to see the faithfulness of God over the course of time.

AFTER THE BALL, Cinderella had to wait for the prince to come to her rescue and make her dreams come true. In the meantime, she continued to live with her wicked stepmother and cruel stepsisters. Floors that needed scrubbing and laundry that needed washing didn't disappear just because she hoped her true love would come one day to take her away from the drudgery of life.

When my life was falling apart, I still had to manage the mundane responsibilities of life while waiting to see if God would come to my rescue. I simply tried to do the best I could do in the circumstances. When Taylor was five months old, I had to go back to work. I accepted a regular job since no position in ministry was open to me. When I became pregnant with our third child, Haley, we decided to move back to southern California.

Pat's new job as a manager with a major restaurant chain was what we needed financially. But the stress of relocating and the demands of Pat's job put tremendous pressures on me. I knew no one. I had a six-year-old, a one-year-old, and a baby on the way. Pat worked an unpredictable schedule, upwards of sixty hours each week. His typical workday began at four-thirty in the afternoon, and he'd get off work sometime after three in the morning. Since we only had one car, I had to drive him to work and pick him up in the middle of the night if I didn't want to be stranded. During this time, I didn't sleep very well if he did take the car to work—I still struggled with fears that he might not come directly home.

We began counseling as soon as we got settled in our new apartment. Pat started an intense training program with his new company at the same time. He was thoroughly consumed with work. The little time we had together was focused on our counseling and the issues it raised. These were not easy issues to deal with, so our relationship was often strained.

I decided to make use of this season to try to get rid of some old rags from my past. I had never dealt with some of the unresolved issues of my past while I was busy in ministry. Maybe I kept myself busy so I could ignore the pain of the past I carried with me. But now I wanted to break the self-defeating patterns I had relied on. For eighteen months Pat and I continued in counseling, but not just for Pat's problems. I began the sometimes troubling process of working through my issues too.

Pregnancy and childbirth alone are enough to stress any marriage, and ours was no exception. When Haley was born, we had the joy of a new baby but also the responsibility of helping our other two children adapt to having less of Mommy's attention. Pat's demanding schedule didn't get any easier, but whenever he was home, he helped with the kids as much as he could. It was an exhausting time. Pat was doing his best to provide for his family, deal with his own recovery, and also deal with my fears and suspicions. We were still trying to catch up financially from our recent losses. The stress level in our relationship was off the charts.

During this difficult, uneventful season, I did what I knew I needed to do to sustain my faith: I went to church, worshiped God, tried to pray, stayed in relationships with others who loved Jesus, and read the Bible. Although I didn't feel God's love for me, every day that I managed to endure with some degree of joy, I knew I had endured it by the grace of God.

My close friends didn't live nearby, and I kept a safe distance from those who could have become friends. I knew I needed support from people who loved me and loved God, but I didn't want to risk being hurt again as I had been hurt before. I joined a Bible study group for pregnant women and nursing mothers, but I kept the focus off me as much as possible. I was lonely, but unwilling to risk new relationships.

I continued to grow more and more lonely. I relied heavily on Rayna and another dear friend, Kim, for friendship and prayer support, calling them often on the phone. Their faith and friendship buoyed me when I felt uncertain, but it wasn't enough to fill the emotional deficit growing inside me.

I appreciated Pat's dedication to our marriage. Not only was he working hard at dealing with the issues that led to his previous infidelity, but he was also working at a demanding job for the sake of his family. I knew his dedication was born of love, but I didn't feel that love. Instead, I was starving for affection and affirmation. I felt lonely and weary.

Our counselor helped me understand my issues, and she also confronted me with how I had put up walls in my relationship with Pat. She made me realize that I was afraid of being hurt again, afraid to love Pat with my whole heart. I cried out for romance in our relationship, but I didn't dare let myself fall in love with him again. I begged for renewed intimacy, but I cut myself off emotionally whenever Pat tried to be close to me. I was hungry for love, but afraid to deeply satisfy that hunger with my husband as I had done before.

A man I had known for many years, and whom I cared for deeply, came back into my life at that time. He found me attractive, and I found myself attracted to him so strongly that it startled me. He offered closeness without complications. He was someone who didn't remind me of all the problems in my life, someone who was willing to comfort me and distract me from the drudgery and difficult work of a marriage in recovery.

Before this time I never would have believed I could be susceptible to sexual temptation. I always thought I was spiritually exempt from entertaining even the idea of having an affair. I knew an affair would not be right, but I was hungry for love and comfort.

My emptiness left a place for bitterness to take root and grow. I started thinking, *Why should I go on being good when I'm paying the consequences for someone else's sins? I did nothing to bring this about! I remained true to my marriage commitment and true to God, but what did it get me? I'm paying the same price as one who had an affair, but I didn't get any of the pleasure.* I began trying to justify what I knew was wrong, thinking, *Why should I suffer the penalty without having had the "fun" of being passionate with someone? I've already lost everything anyway. What does it matter if I obey God and try to stay on the straight and narrow path?*

Our counselor picked up on my changed attitude. She wanted me to talk out what was going on, but I didn't want to. I knew the things I was saying to myself wouldn't hold up in the light of scrutiny, especially with those who shared my commitment to the Bible. I talked with Pat about my struggles. He tried to warn me, to convince me that the pleasures of sin came with built-in guilt and devastating consequences to follow. He acknowledged my hunger, but assured me that while sin may taste good for a moment, it would leave me with a greater hunger after it was over.

I had to decide how I would satisfy my hunger. If I gave up my flirtation with this affair, I would have to risk intimacy with Pat again. It was not an easy decision, even though I knew the right thing to do.

I made the decision to talk about my struggle with a few trusted friends whose faith and wisdom I admired. Each one basically said the same things, the things I didn't need anyone to tell me because it was what I had counseled others when I knew nothing of the kind of hunger I knew now. Most importantly, my friends prayed with me and for me during this time of temptation. More than once, when my resolve faltered, circumstances intervened to keep me from falling into sin. I believe God was at work through the prayers of my husband and my friends.

I learned something important about sin and temptation during this struggle: Sin appeals to us most when it addresses a real need in our lives. I've heard it said that sin is an illegitimate way of trying to fill a legitimate need. The hunger inside me was legitimate, but I had to decide if I would risk the intimacy required to fill that hunger in the right way, or if I would revert to the old rags of trying to fill my need in an illegitimate way.

Would I choose to follow God's lead by obeying his commands, or would I revert to my old rags by going my own way? I struggled with this decision. I wavered more than once. But when I had to decide, I chose to obey God and remain faithful to my husband. In the final analysis, I knew my best hope for intimacy and true fulfillment would come by following God's lead. I knew that a satisfying love relationship with a man came in the context of marriage.

Even though I had based my decision on faith in God's Word, I didn't feel that great afterwards. I struggled with feelings of sadness and fear. At times I even felt angry, because my needs weren't immediately filled. But I truly believed that my choice to obey God would eventually be rewarded.

• • •

AFTER OUR FAMILY MOVED to Sacramento, our lives became easier. The two little ones finally grew out of diapers, we bought a second car, and we found a church attended by a couple who had been our friends in northern California. They had moved to Sacramento before us and were able to introduce us to some of their friends from church.

Then another couple who knew us from northern California moved to the Sacramento area to plant a new church. An opportunity arose for us to help start a youth ministry in our neighborhood. The pastor knew of our past, but he wanted our help anyway.

Pat had completed the requirements for restoration given him by the church board, but he hadn't pursued having the restrictions on his ministry lifted because there had been no reason for him to do so. My hopes were rekindled. I had always believed full restoration would include youth ministry again on some level. With my encouragement, Pat wrote to the chairman of the church board. He explained the situation and asked them to fulfill their commitment to lift the ministry ban they had imposed four years earlier.

They responded with a request that we prove Pat had fulfilled his part of the commitment. Pat mailed them verification of his compliance. By the time these letters went back and forth, the couple planting the new church decided to move to another area to accept a position at an established church. My dreams of doing youth ministry again were back on hold. Sometime later Pat received a letter rescinding the restrictions placed on his ministry. The members of the church board encouraged Pat and seemed genuinely happy to hear he was thinking about serving God in youth ministry again. They didn't mention me in the letter. When we had asked previously about a restoration plan for me, they had said that I didn't need restoration because I hadn't sinned. I felt left out and hurt all over again when they didn't mention me in the letter of restoration.

While reading through a portion of the Old Testament, I came across a verse where God spoke of taking David from the sheep pasture and making him a king. I felt as if I had been put out to pasture and forgotten there. Would the same God who didn't leave David out in the pasture remember me and come to my rescue too? I wrote the verse in my prayer journal, along with how I was feeling about the letter.

On Sunday, the pastor at our new church preached on the very same verse. This seemed more than mere coincidence! I hoped he would make some application that addressed my heart. Then he said something to the effect that he believed God wanted him to give a specific word of encouragement to someone there that day, someone whom men had removed from a ministry, but these men wouldn't acknowledge it. "God wants you to know this," the pastor said. "Today God himself has reinstated you."

I had my prayer journal in my hand. I opened it and reread what I had written earlier that week. After the service, I showed the pastor. Pat and I didn't know what to make of this pronouncement. We knew of no opportunities to minister. We spoke to the youth pastor there to see if he needed extra volunteers. He didn't. I offered to work with the junior high kids. Again I was told they didn't need any more help. Apparently the pronouncement had been preparation for something in the future.

This experience encouraged me that God did indeed care. I grew more confident he would fulfill his promises. I didn't force the issue. Pat and I focused on taking care of our own children, spending more time together, and developing our relationship, which was improving dramatically. I also focused on the opportunities God gave me to write. Pat was still working the crazy schedule of a restaurant manager and could come to church with us only on rare occasions. We continued to pray for God to release Pat from this kind of schedule that interfered with his spiritual growth and our family life.

Not only was Pat robbed figuratively of time with us, but he was also robbed at gunpoint three times while on the job. I prayed fervently that God would come through in some tangible way to release us from the financial necessity of Pat's stressful job and help us find somewhere we could work together once more. We tried to find better alternatives, but again we had to wait for the salvation of God.

We went on with our lives, doing the chores, meeting the children's needs, and tending the hearth of our family life, but also living with the assurance that God hadn't forgotten us. If God hadn't forgotten my dreams that had come true only to disappear, maybe he would help us reach the dreams we were daring to dream together again. We were sure that God would come to our rescue at the right time, even though we had no idea when that time might come. In the meantime, we determined to be content.

ELEVEN

The Strength and Dignity of the Princess Bride

Respecting your position, understanding your privileges, and wielding power wisely

CINDERELLA HELD ON TO her remaining glass slipper, hoping that her prince would find her and take her away to live happily ever after. In a few days, the prince came for her, and they were married right away.

By marrying the prince, Princess Ella (the former Cinderella) became the daughter-in-law to the king and a joint heir to the throne. As princess, she received favored status and the privilege of making requests of the king. Being in a respected position, understanding her privileges, and feeling the love surrounding her must have given this transformed servant-girl a sense of her own dignity. Because of this dignity and the kindness in her heart, she never used her position as an opportunity to put others down; rather, she held her own head high while she lifted others up. In one version of the fairy tale, Princess Ella was so kindhearted that she used her position and power to arrange good marriages for her cruel stepsisters with members of the court.

Those of us who accept the love of God gain a spiritual position, and with that position, strength and dignity. However, just because you enter the kingdom of God (or the kingdom of God enters you, which ever way you choose to look at it), doesn't mean others will start treating you with the respect you deserve. If you want to receive the respect God intends for his Princess Bride, you must first respect the love God has demonstrated toward you and internalize what that love says about you. Once you treat yourself with respect, you will be able to exercise the authority God has given you by using your strength and dignity to set firm boundaries regarding treatment that degrades you or disavows the dignity you rightfully deserve as a woman chosen by God.

God's kingdom is a foreign power in this earthly realm. Even Jesus said his kingdom is not of this world. The Bible says, "We know that we are children of God, and that the whole world is under the control of the evil one" (1 John 5:19). When we begin to understand and exercise our power and privileges in the spiritual realm, we will not go unchallenged.

The forces of evil do not take lightly one who begins to pray to her Father in heaven, "Thy Kingdom come, Thy will be done, on earth as it is in heaven." Spiritual forces of wickedness despise those who dare try to exert the authority of the heavenly kingdom on this earthly one. When challenges come, you must be prepared to stand firm in your faith and exercise the authority God has given you.

ONE OF MY OWN encounters with this kind of spiritual struggle occurred on the train ride back to school after going to Oregon to visit my mom. The trip took nearly twenty hours because the train made frequent stops. During the night I couldn't sleep. I kept thinking about Mom's alcoholism, praying for her, and fighting off worry. I wasn't thinking clearly about much else and didn't feel much like making small talk with the other passengers; besides, now that we were in the wee hours of the morning, most of the other passengers were asleep.

At Sacramento I got off the train to get a cup of hot chocolate at the station. As I stepped down from the steps, a police officer took me by the arm. "Excuse me, miss," said the officer. "Are you traveling alone?"

"Yes."

"Then I advise that you get right back on the train. Several young girls have been reported missing recently from the train stations. We suspect they are being kidnapped by a pimp. There's quite a problem with drugs and prostitution."

"But I just wanted to get a hot drink . . ."

He was of an imposing height, but with a kind face that now seemed impatient with my naivete. "Miss, I advise you to get right back on the train. You can get a hot drink later. My job is to make sure we don't lose any more young girls like yourself."

So I got back on the train and scrunched uncomfortably back in my seat. I tried to sleep until daylight came, but sleep escaped me. We came to the Fresno station at about 4 A.M. Now I wanted that hot chocolate more than ever, so I got off the train with a few other passengers and went into the coffee shop. The others sat together in pairs without paying any attention to me. I bought my hot chocolate and sat down at the cleanest table I could find.

When I looked up, I noticed a man in the doorway whom I had not seen on the train. His gaze surveyed the scene and fixed on me. He was a tall thin man, smartly dressed in a black fedora, black slacks, and a black shirt under a black trench coat. Now, I did not know what a pimp looked like; before the police officer's warning at the previous stop, I had never given the matter any thought. What I did know was that this man was definitely out of place here, and he was walking intently in my direction. I dropped my gaze and sent up a silent prayer. The man sat down at my little table without speaking a word.

"Excuse me . . ." I said, more out of shock than anything else.

He smiled, exhibiting confidence. "You don't mind if I sit here, do you?"

I heard myself say "No," as my mind raced, trying to figure out what to do. The others from the train were intent on their sleepy conversations, taking no notice of me. The man was attractive: he had dark, flawless skin, captivating eyes, and a sly, confident smile. He wore a diamond ring on the little finger of his left hand. The fingernail of the little finger on his right hand was longer than the rest.

He wasted no time getting to the purpose of his little visit.

"You are a beautiful lady. Has anyone ever told you the kind of love waiting for ladies like you? I could fix you up good. I could show you love like you have never known. I could make you fly."

"Excuse me, I'm not interested. I'm not that kind of girl."

He laughed softly, incredulously. Then he slowly took out a pack of cigarettes from his shirt pocket, took out a cigarette, lit it, and drew on it deeply, never taking his gaze off me. It reminded me of how a snake tries to mesmerize its prey with its eyes.

"They are all that kind of girl when I get done with them."

At that, I stood up, intending to make a dash for the door. He grabbed my arm, pulling me down into the chair. I looked around for help, but the counter person was gone and the other passengers were outside.

Something inside me snapped to attention. Who did this man think he was? How dare he touch me and insinuate such vile things! Maybe it was the association in my mind with the snake, but I now clearly saw this stand off as a matter of the kingdom of darkness versus the kingdom of light. I suddenly remembered who I was and who I served and the verse that promised, "God has given you authority to trample on snakes and scorpions, and to overcome all the power of the evil one." Well, as far as I could see, this guy was a snake, and I was certain I would win this encounter.

I'm sure the Holy Spirit must have taken over at that point, turning my fear into some other kind of energy and telling me what to say. I shook his hand loose from my arm, put my shoulders back, and raised my head, no longer willing to cower before the likes of him.

"Sir, obviously you don't know who I am."

"Say, what?" he said quizzically.

"I said, obviously you don't know who I am or who my father is, because if you did, you wouldn't dare talk to me the way you've been talking to me."

"Who . . . who's your father?"

"God is my father, and he doesn't stand for anyone talking to his daughter like that. What is your name, sir?"

"My name is Samuel. Why?"

"Well, Samuel, I have a few things to tell you. You may think you came in here for one reason, but I happen to know that you came in here for another reason. You see, my life is dedicated to God. I'm his, and as long as I live on this earth, I am an ambassador for his kingdom of love, true love, not the kind of smut you call love. You thought you came in here to show me what real love is—well, you're wrong, mister. You came in here so I could show *you* what real love is."

He looked shocked, but I didn't give him a chance to seize control again. I just kept right on talking.

"You aren't talking about love," I continued. "Love has four letters in the word. What you were talking about only has three letters: S-I-N. But, Samuel, God must have mercy on you because he sent you here to meet me. And God knows that every day when I get up I pray, 'Lord, if there is someone who needs to know your love today, bring them my way so I can share your love with them.' Well, Samuel, you are the one God brought to me today, so I am going to do my part."

I quickly reached into my bag and brought out a tract called "The Four Spiritual Laws," that I had been taught to use to lead someone to understand God's love for them and their need to surrender to him. I hurried to read it, because while the tables had turned, I was still aware that I did not want to miss boarding the train before it left the station.

"Law number one: Samuel, God loves you and has a wonderful plan for your life." He was actually reading along in the booklet as I turned each page and read the Bible verses telling him that his sins had separated him from God, that God sent Jesus to die on the cross to pay for every sin he had ever committed, and that he must choose to accept the free gift of God in Christ Jesus.

"Will you pray this prayer with me now? Will you accept the real love God is offering you this night?" Samuel looked at me with a puzzled expression, as though he didn't know whether to laugh or cry. Then he just shook his head. He didn't say another word.

"Look, Samuel, it was nice to meet you, but I have to go catch my train. I want you to keep this little booklet. You may not be ready to receive God's love now, but maybe someday you will. God loves you. He really does."

I started to walk away, leaving him sitting there next to the now cold cocoa, holding a little gold tract in his hand. When I reached the door, now confident I would make it back to the train, I couldn't resist saying one last thing.

"Samuel—"

He looked up at me.

"Does your mother know what you do?"

Knowing who I am and whose I am gave me real power in a high-stakes power struggle that night between the kingdom of darkness and the kingdom of light. I dare not think what might have happened if I had forgotten my authority in God's kingdom, the privilege of prayer, and the purpose of my life.

CONFLICTS WITH THOSE oblivious to our spiritual stature are usually far less dramatic than this one. Usually they take the form of day-to-day putdowns, jabs, comments, and actions that degrade the beauty of your soul and the sovereignty of your spirit as you try your best to live a better life. You may have become accustomed to being treated this way, especially by members of your family or others with whom you have grown up. It seems that those who knew you before you entered into your position of spiritual strength are the least likely to affirm your prosperity of spirit. Jesus himself said, "No prophet is accepted in his hometown." But Jesus didn't let the people he grew up with keep him down, and you don't have to either. To do so is to show disrespect for the position God has given you.

Britain's Prince Charles stood on an open stage before a large crowd for a public appearance in 1994. During the assembly, a would-be attacker stormed the stage, aiming for Prince Charles. While the attacker was wrestled to the ground, the prince calmly stepped aside. The British press noted with pride how Prince Charles had carried himself with dignity under the circumstances. Remind yourself often that you are the bride of the prince, daughter to the King of the universe. You may or may not be able to stop someone's attack from reaching you, but you can learn to step out of the way and handle any situation with dignity.

If you cannot distance yourself physically from the would-be attacker, you can still deflect the arrows aimed at you before they lodge in your heart and mind where they can do you damage. You do this by learning to put up an invisible shield, the shield of faith in God's promises and pronouncements about your value in his kingdom. Whenever someone begins to tear you down, stop the picture in your mind. Remind yourself that their behavior and words reveal more about them than they do about you. Don't buy into their message that says you are less than God says you are. Don't receive it. Don't agree with it. Don't accept it. Don't succumb to it. When you respect yourself in this way, you retain your dignity.

There is a kingdom of darkness and a kingdom of light. You cannot shut off the darkness of the world or make everyone good, but you *can* bring light and truth and goodness wherever you are by bringing God's Spirit into the situation and by behaving as God would have you behave. Always remember that you are an ambassador of God's kingdom, sent out to spread good will wherever you go, even if you find yourself in situations where people do not recognize your King or his authority.

AS I PREPARED TO LEAVE college, Pat and I had been praying about what direction our lives should take. I had an interest in youth work but no opportunities for a paid position. Pat had a degree in music and longed to pursue a career in musical theater. I admire Pat's talent, and at that time I wanted to do all I could to encourage his pursuit of a professional career that would make good use of his talents. We put our career decisions before God in prayer and asked him to guide us.

We agreed that the only way Pat could pursue a career in theater would be for me to find a job paying roughly four times what I made working in the Career Planning and Placement office at Pepperdine. We prayed that if it was okay for Pat to pursue this dream, God would show us by giving me a job where I could make that specific amount of money. If that happened, we would know it was the Lord, because the amount was more than double the average starting salaries for recent college grads.

To effectively teach a seminar at the career center, I demonstrated how to find a job you could love by going through the process myself and then reporting back to the students in the seminar. While doing informational interviews with several employment agencies, I found myself genuinely enthusiastic about what employment counselors did in their work. I loved the thought of meeting new people, interviewing them, and helping direct them to possible jobs. I enjoyed the challenge of gaining the trust of prospective employers, selling them on the benefits an applicant could provide their business, and helping their business grow by finding the right applicants for the job. It seemed like a good way to use my natural abilities to provide a valuable service.

The counselor with whom I spoke initially tried to discourage me. She said she worked at a highly competitive office, one of the best in the business. They only kept counselors who could produce results. These things only fueled my interest. Then she gave me the clincher: "We work on straight commission. In fact, we only keep counselors who earn a particular amount each month."

When I asked her what that amount was, it was the exact amount Pat and I had prayed for.

When I finally was given an appointment with the manager, she did her best to explain why I couldn't do the job. I met her every objection with valid examples of previous performance that demonstrated I could do the job. It was a wrestling match of beliefs: she didn't believe I could do it, and I believed, with God's help, I could. She finally gave me the job because she said it was the only way she could prove to me that I couldn't do it. She was wrong. I placed two applicants in positions during my first week on the job.

She had been correct, however, in that I didn't realize what I was getting myself into. Two weeks after she hired me, the entire staff—one hundred counselors and their guests—was invited to a weekend-long company anniversary party held at a hotel owned by the woman who founded the company. It also happened to be the weekend of our first wedding anniversary.

We thanked God for the free anniversary celebration and drove out to Palm Springs. When we arrived, I caught a glimpse of what my manager, Geneva, had tried to warn me about. She saw me as this twenty-one-year-old Christian girl entering into a world of hard-drinking, cutthroat, female barracudas. She had a point! Although I accepted and appreciated most of the women in the office (the men hired were not able to maintain performance up to the standard and never lasted very long), they were a rowdy bunch.

When we arrived, Geneva proudly dragged me up to meet the company president. Geneva was now touting me as her greatest discovery. The president was beautifully dressed, draped in diamonds, and thoroughly drunk. She wanted to know how much I had had to pay to get this boy—referring to Pat—to sleep with me for the weekend. She refused to believe we were married and tried to convince us there was no need to keep up such a pretense. Another drunk co-worker pulled Pat out onto the dance floor and told him, in vivid phrases peppered with four-letter words, that I was one of the best blankety-blank counselors she had ever seen. Nearly every woman brought a "friend" along; some brought male lovers, though I found out that weekend that many of them were lesbians and that their female friends were more than friends.

Understanding my position in God's kingdom helped me be a light in a situation Geneva thought I wouldn't be able to handle. I wasn't there to make judgments on their lives. I was there as an answer to prayer so Pat could pursue his heart's desires and so I could be an ambassador of God's love. So I politely drank sodas, retired early with my husband, gratefully enjoyed the generosity of our host, and had a beautiful weekend in Palm Springs. I also began to pray with greater understanding that God would give me a chance to share the message of God's love with these women I was growing to care for more and more with each passing week.

I continued to excel at work, consistently billing the required amount. In October of 1980 I won the honor of being Counselor of the Month, billing more than anyone in the entire company of thirteen offices. Although I didn't have many opportunities to meet with top management on a personal basis where I might find an opportunity to share with any of them about spiritual issues, the Lord *had* orchestrated several situations in which those in my office saw God on the move and asked me to explain my faith. Unless asked, I didn't force my views on anyone. I just kept their respect by working hard and achieving good results.

As the time approached for the next annual weekend bash in Palm Springs, I felt drawn to pray more consistently for a chance to talk to the company president about God's love for her. By now I had gained the respect of my co-workers as a seasoned counselor, one of only four women in our office who had held their positions for an entire year. I had also grown to like and respect the women with whom I worked, regardless of the stark contrasts in our chosen lifestyles.

When we arrived in Palm Springs once again, I was easily accepted. Pat and I enjoyed the party, celebrating our anniversary again and staying up late with the rest of the group. Pat finally got tired and went back to our room when the party moved from the restaurant to the pool at two in the morning. By now, most of those remaining were sufficiently drunk so that there was little inhibition left in them. It was obvious to me that some of them were shamelessly fawning over the president to impress themselves upon her. I was staying close for another reason. I felt a deep conviction that God wanted to call her to himself. I didn't intend to try to talk to her while she was drunk, but I thought that I might find an opportunity to suggest we get together at another time to discuss work.

By four in the morning there were about fifteen of us left. Several women draped their arms around each other, sitting in the jacuzzi, loudly singing every folk song they could remember. The president started singing "I Don't Know How to Love Him" from the rock-opera *Jesus Christ Superstar*. I tried to hide my chagrin when they wailed the part about, "He's a man. He's just a man . . ."

Then the president stopped the song and said, "That makes me cry. It's so beautiful how Jesus was Mary's lover. It's so beautiful that he didn't reject her because she was a prostitute."

I almost choked at that, praying silently, "Okay, Lord, am I supposed to try to correct the heretical theology of a drunken woman at four in the morning? I don't think so! Lord, help. What am I supposed to do here?"

Then she said, "Let's sing 'Amazing Grace.' I love that song." They dutifully tried to fulfill her request, but it was pitiful at best.

Then one woman from my office interjected, "Hey, Connie, you must know that one." So, on request, I sang three verses of the hymn "Amazing Grace," while my inebriated choir came in on the chorus. After that, it was somehow decided that we had to give the Jewish tradition equal honor and we all crawled out of the jacuzzi, tied towels around us, interlocked arms, and began doing a wobbly version of the hora while singing "Hava Nagila."

What happened next took me by total surprise and gave me a glimpse of my spiritual authority that I had not understood before.

The company president looked at me directly. It was as though a light went on inside her. She stopped laughing and seemed to sober up. The eight or nine others still with us stopped laughing too. She fixed her gaze on me and said, "You have the call of God on your life. I can see it on you. You have the call of God on your life. You are fired. Don't come back to the office on Monday."

Everyone was utterly shocked. Tears formed in Geneva's eyes.

I asked the president, "What does God's call on my life have to do with whether or not I work for you?"

She replied, "God called me once, and I turned away from his call. I don't want to have anything to do with keeping anyone else from following his call. I'm sorry, but you're fired."

That broke the little party up—quickly. Once the president of the company started firing people, no one wanted to be within reach. I went immediately back to our room, woke Pat to pray with me, and told him what had happened. By the time we went out for brunch, my dismissal and the unusual pronouncement was the talk of the entire company. Geneva wanted to take me to the president's room so we could talk some sense into her. I too wanted to talk to her, but I understood our standoff to be of a spiritual nature rather than a practical, earthly one. Pat continued to pray as Geneva and I went to her room. On the way, Geneva told me that the president could "see things in the spiritual realm" because she practiced white witchcraft. She also assured me that the president loved Christ and the Bible.

Once in the room, Geneva pointed out that it was entirely illegal for the president to fire me because of my religious convictions. Since the president was no longer under the influence of alcohol, she agreed to discuss the matter more rationally. She said to me, "Connie, there is a call of God on your life, isn't there?"

"Well, yes," I answered. "But my call is to be a light wherever God sends me. I believe he sent me here to be a light to many people who would never go to a church. I don't want to hide away from the world, cloistered away with others who believe exactly as I do. I can go anywhere because I am confident of my position in God's kingdom."

She asked me if I would be willing to resign. She seemed truly concerned that she would somehow be held guilty if I missed the call of God on my life.

I explained that I too wanted to fulfill the call of God, and for the time being I was called to bring God's message to her. Therefore, I couldn't even consider resigning until I had fulfilled the purpose of sharing God's message with her.

Her face brightened. "I see what you are saying. You're saying that Jesus is your power base. I see, Jesus gives you a power base. Wow, that's great! I never thought of that before. You have to tell the others!" Now she seemed genuinely excited. I don't know what she meant exactly when she said "Jesus gives you a power base," but she kept repeating it with wonder in her voice.

She made me wait there while she called an immediate meeting of all her top brass, managers, and assistant managers. Once they were assembled in her suite, she told them, "I just learned the most amazing thing from Connie. Jesus is her power base. Now she is going to tell us all about it." I couldn't believe the turn of events. Here these women, for whom I had been praying for over a year, were commanded by their boss to sit down and let me share with them what I knew of the love of God, God's kingdom, and the authority I had as an ambassador for his kingdom. All the while the company president smiled and nodded her head affirmingly.

As I was leaving, I thanked her for letting me keep my job and suggested that maybe she and I could talk more since we seemed to have come to an agreement. Her countenance changed and she said to me, "I know who you are and you know who I am, so let's not play games."

After that strange confrontation, I decided I had fulfilled the call of God on my life at that company. Within six months I moved to another position, but I have never since forgotten that we truly do wield spiritual power and authority. In that case it took someone from the other side, recognizing who I was, to remind me that spiritual kingdoms are real, and those who serve in them do so to real effect.

CERTAIN PRIVILEGES ARE AFFORDED to us in our position as Princess Bride. By making good use of these privileges, we gain access to the power, strength, and wealth of God, to be put to use on our behalf.

The privilege of wearing the robes of righteousness. Isaiah 61:10 says, "I delight greatly in the LORD; my soul rejoices in my God.

For he has clothed me with garments of salvation and arrayed me in a robe of righteousness, as a bridegroom adorns his head like a priest, and as a bride adorns herself with her jewels."

This robe is not our own good works that cover us and make us right with God. Isaiah 64:6 tells us that "our righteous acts are like filthy rags." God took us as we were and purchased righteousness for us so that we can stand fully acceptable before him.

The privilege of calling God "Abba." "Abba" is baby talk for Father. It is the term a young Hebrew child utters as their first word, like Dada or Papa. It is a fond and affectionate term that is only appropriate for use by family. Romans 8:15–17 tells us, "You received the Spirit of sonship. And by him we cry, 'Abba, Father.' The Spirit himself testifies with our spirit that we are God's children. Now if we are children, then we are heirs—heirs of God and co-heirs with Christ, if indeed we share in his sufferings in order that we may also share in his glory."

The privilege of making petition directly to the king. Think of the incredible privilege a little girl has when she can crawl up on her daddy's knee and ask anything she wants of him. Now add to this picture the understanding that her daddy has unlimited resources, power, and a wealth of wisdom. This is the privilege provided by the gift of prayer to the Princess Bride.

Jesus explained the privilege bestowed on those who enter into this "Abba" relationship with God the Father through being united with him. He said, "In that day you will no longer ask me anything. I tell you the truth, my Father will give you whatever you ask in my name. Until now you have not asked for anything in my name. Ask and you will receive, and your joy will be complete. In that day [after Jesus' resurrection] you will ask in my name" (John 16:23–24, 26).

If you live your life dancing in the arms of God by maintaining an intimate relationship with Jesus Christ and following his lead, you are in a position of tremendous power. This is not only personal power through greater self-confidence, but also supernatural power through the privilege of prayer. Jesus gives us the right to go directly to God the Father and ask anything. Of course, when we are dancing in the arms of God, we will only ask for things that are in keeping with God's will.

Imagine a bride dressed in rich and glorious robes of righteousness, brought before the king by her husband the prince. The king welcomes her, embraces her, and says to her, "Because you love my son, whisper whatever you want in my ear and I will do it for you." I suppose this is the "power base" my employer spoke of with such awe and respect, our intimate access to God and all his mighty resources. We are not to use these resources frivolously, but wisely, for good and not evil.

When we remember who we are and who we represent, our demeanor will instantly change. We will not often get carried away by the urgent rush of emotions that may cause us to be less than dignified. And if we do get carried away, it takes only a glimpse of who we are in our position in God's kingdom to restore our dignity.

My daughter Haley, who is three, alternately uses whining and tantrum-throwing as her primary means of power. Because she has limited communications skills and is the youngest and weakest of the three siblings, whining and throwing tantrums are her most effective means of getting attention and action from people who have more power than she does.

One day when things were not going my way, I noticed a similarity between my behavior and Haley's. I caught myself vacillating between two modes: the helpless, whining, "please-pity-me-

and-come-to-my-rescue" mode, and the tantrum-throwing "if-I-can't-get-my-way-I'm-going-to-make-sure-someone-suffers-for-my-inconvenience" mode. At this point, God interrupted my thoughts. "What are you so upset about?" he seemed to be asking me. "Why are you acting this way?"

I was acting like Haley because I was feeling powerless over my circumstances. I realized that strength and dignity are not within reach of the immature or those who feel powerless. Instead, those who feel powerless rely on the manipulations of weakness: playing the martyr, whining, blaming others, throwing tantrums, or having outbursts of anger. Now that I clearly saw my error, I prayed for the Lord to give me another way to approach the situation. I needed to see myself in the light of my royal position and the privileges that come with it.

Whenever we find ourselves acting without strength and dignity, we must stop and ask ourselves: "Do I have a relationship with Almighty God? Am I living as one in my position might live? Am I using my privileges and wielding the power God has given me?" If not, stop. Remind yourself of who you are and who you represent, and let God change your attitude. Then you can tap into the privileges that are yours and wield power wisely.

Proverbs 31:25 says this about an excellent woman: "She is clothed with strength and dignity; she can laugh at the days to come." When we practice respecting our position, making good use of our privileges, and wielding power wisely, the same will be said of us. Strength and dignity will be our clothing, and we will laugh at the days to come, waiting patiently and with assurance of a "happily ever after" just beyond the bend.

TWELVE

Until Happily Ever After ...

Waiting for the perfect ending

At the end of the story, Cinderella and her prince lived happily ever after. When we get to the end of our story, we too will live happily ever after. But that end, for us, cannot come until the Prince of Peace enforces his rule as King of Kings over all the kingdoms of this earth. In the meantime, we continue to seek personal fulfillment and intimacy with God by following his lead.

While I accept that we can't live happily ever after here and now, I am grateful for the happiness I have. There were times I wasn't sure if I would ever be happy again, but I am today because God has been a faithful partner in this dance of life. He was the one who promised a crown of beauty instead of ashes, gladness instead of mourning, a garment of praise instead of a spirit of despair. I made no mistake when I believed him enough to hope for all of these.

By continuing to follow God's lead, I am finding the power to change, the courage to live freely, and the inspiration to reach for my dreams—not just in some spiritual fantasy world but in real life. Until "happily ever after" comes, life can still be rich and good as we live to see God fulfill our Cinderella aspirations.

There are flowers growing in my backyard where there was only dirt a year ago. The bulbs we planted way back when have sprouted, blossomed, faded, and grown up to blossom again with the coming of spring. The lilies are getting ready to bloom, and little yellow flowers that look like the kind of trumpets angels sound peek out from beneath them. We have to keep pulling weeds in order to keep the beauty of the flowers in sight, but it's worth the work.

Every time I look out my kitchen window, I am reminded that beauty is hidden all around us, waiting to be brought forth. It takes faith to believe in the beauty and perseverance to make sure the weeds don't obscure it, but my hope is renewed as springtime brings new life. I'm going to continue planting flower bulbs. I'm also going to continue nurturing the beauty I trust is within me and in others. I'm going to face the challenges that threaten to obscure that beauty, and I'm going to accept each season of growth as it comes.

I read this anonymous bit of wisdom in a popular women's magazine: "When I was a little girl, I was dying to grow up and go to school. When I was in high school, I was dying to finish school and go on to college. When I was in college, I was dying to graduate so I could marry and start a family. When I married and had young children, I was dying for them to grow up so I could get some rest. My children grew up, moved away. I just found out I am dying and realize that I have never lived."

Until "happily ever after," I want to live each day and each moment as fully as I can. I want to aspire to live a balanced life, not despising any of my roles or responsibilities, but doing whatever I do to the glory of God, whether that is writing a book or wiping a runny nose. This balancing act is not easy, as any woman knows. We have much to juggle while we try to stay focused on what takes priority at each moment.

One of my children's favorite books is called *Mirette On the High Wire*. I can relate to Mirette's story. Mirette is a young girl of about twelve who lives with her mother in turn-of-the-century Paris. Her mother is an innkeeper who hosts many famous traveling performers. One of their guests is the Great Bellini, a high-wire walker who has lost his nerve. Mirette secretly watches Bellini practice walking on a wire raised above their patio. One day she dares to ask Bellini to teach her to walk on the wire. He discourages her, saying, "Once you walk on the wire, your feet will never be happy on the ground."

Mirette replies, "My feet are already unhappy on the ground."

Mirette practices on her own and refuses to give up although she falls many times. She keeps it up until she can make it across the wire. Then Bellini agrees to teach her. He tells her the secret to keeping her balance is to "think only of the wire and of crossing to the end." At the end of the story, the Great Bellini attempts to perform again before an audience. He secures a wire across the square from the rooftop of Mirette's mother's inn. When he steps out on the wire, he freezes for a moment. Mirette runs up several flights of stairs and steps out onto the wire, approaching her mentor from the other side. Together they cross the sky, thinking only of the wire and of crossing to the end.

This is a picture of how I try to live my daily life. God is with me on the wire. He has watched me try and try again to keep my balance, and has encouraged my perseverance. I have learned that I make the most progress whenever I focus on what I have committed myself to at the moment, whether that be playing with my kids, completing a writing assignment, helping out at school, paying bills, rinsing the dishes, or making love to my husband. I also set goals in all areas of my life and seek to balance them—not by trying to accomplish them all at once, but by respecting each area of my life enough to give it my full attention at the appropriate time.

I have also learned to juggle a few things while I focus on whatever takes priority. In this way, I satisfy my desire to go higher, and I do more in life without missing out like the woman who found she was dying and realized she had never lived.

RECENTLY, AUTHOR, INTERIOR DESIGNER, and lifestyle advocate Alexandra Stoddard was scheduled to give a lecture in our area on "Making Choices for a Beautiful Life." I had read several of her books and found her writings inspirational. I wrestled over whether to attend the lecture; I was working to meet a deadline, and many other things were pressing for my attention.

I finally decided to go because I felt as though I needed to do something to nurture myself. Alexandra's slide presentation featured beautiful homes and elegant rooms, all beautifully decorated. Part of me wanted to shout, "Yes! That's how I want to live!" Another part of me cautioned, "Connie, don't get your hopes up; you know you can't live like that." She encouraged us to invest in creating a place where we could enjoy living our lives beautifully. When her lecture came to a close, a mental tug-of-war began. Part of me wanted to let my aspirations lead me, but another part of me wanted to discourage those aspirations because I feared being dissatisfied if I let myself aspire to live a more beautiful life.

I drove out of the hotel parking lot at the corner of 16th and H streets. Sixteenth street is the only street that leads to the freeway I take to get home, so I turned out of the parking lot onto the dark street, aiming for the freeway. In my mental tug-of-war, I was now leaning in the direction of allowing myself the luxury of aspiring to someday make our home as comfortable and beautiful as I dreamed it could be. Then I noticed something was wrong. I should have been to the freeway by now, but instead I was in a part of town I'd never seen before. I looked carefully at the street signs and realized I was on H street, near 33rd. I had pulled out of a different side of the parking lot than the one I entered and headed mistakenly in the wrong direction.

Then the Lord gave me insight, not just about my driving, but about the issues I struggled with in my heart. I knew I had to turn around, go back to where I started, and turn the right direction in order to get home. God helped me realize that this might be good advice for my life, too. I shouldn't give up just because I spent much of my life going in directions other than where my heart truly aspired to go.

In the time God has given us on this earth, we each have time to encourage the true aspirations of our hearts. This means dreaming of a brighter future, regardless of how dark our past. We have the opportunity to learn from our mistakes. When we realize that we don't want to go in the direction we've been heading, God has provided us with valuable information about where we do want to go and how to get there. While waiting for the perfect ending, we have time to turn around and go in new directions.

Never let yourself stay discouraged or stop aspiring to a better life. Dare to believe your heartfelt desires are valid and your dreams worthwhile. You are free to live out your dreams with all the energy and ingenuity within you as long as you stay within the firm boundaries of God's revealed moral will. Set out to do what you deeply and truly want to do. And if you find that you aren't going to get there by the way you are going, adjust your course.

I WANT TO SPEND my time here on earth allowing God's light to shine through my life. I love Isaiah's prophecy, in 61:3, that God wants to use us to display his splendor. God looks at us and sees a special treasure, a priceless jewel that he wants to use to reflect his own light and beauty. Malachi 3:17 tells us, "'They will be mine,' says the Lord Almighty, 'in the day when I make up my treasured possession.'" Part of our purpose while waiting for the perfect ending is to let God's light shine through the unique jewel that each of our lives represents.

I never paid much attention to jewelry while growing up. I've never worn much jewelry, and I didn't even want a diamond when I got married. My friend Rayna has beautiful rings, one with a large solitaire diamond, another with a row of tiny rubies between two rows of diamonds. I never paid much attention to other women's jewelry, but Rayna is such a close friend and her rings are so pretty, I can't help noticing them.

During a counseling session several years ago, when we lived in southern California, our counselor noticed I didn't have a diamond wedding ring; I had just a simple gold band. She wanted to know why I didn't have a diamond. When I told her that I had never wanted a diamond, she took the issue further.

I had spent over a year in weekly counseling sessions with this counselor, so she knew me fairly well by this time. She was right in guiding me to see that perhaps my disclaimer that "I didn't want a diamond ring" spoke more about my lack of self-respect than my taste in jewelry. When she probed further, I told her that I had always felt as if a diamond would look out of place on my hand. Perhaps I never let myself want a diamond because I thought that the little girl who couldn't wear white didn't deserve a diamond either. The counselor gave me much to ponder and sent me home.

The following week I met Rayna in northern California with plans to drive to Sacramento. Before we left, I told her about my conversation with my counselor regarding my lack of a diamond and lack of interest in having one. Rayna assured me with sincere love that it was okay *not* to want a diamond; however, if Angie was right in her estimation that the reason I didn't want a diamond was because I felt unworthy to wear one, then something must be done.

Rayna set upon a plan she called Jewelry Therapy. She proposed that I wear her rings during our long drive. I could let my true appreciation of their beauty grow as I became more comfortable with them. I felt silly, but I put her rings on my fingers. Every time I looked down at my hand, the sight of those beautiful jewels startled me. They looked so . . . BIG. Rayna assured me that as you wear them longer they actually do get smaller. So we laughed and talked and looked at my hand adorned with jewels. By the end of the trip, Rayna's jewelry therapy session had its intended effect. I came to realize that maybe, someday, I might entertain the idea of having a diamond ring to go with my wedding band.

Over the next several months I started noticing diamonds in the windows of jewelry stores in the mall. Then several months later Pat and I started going into the jewelry stores, looking at the rings in the case. While we were browsing one day, a gemologist gave us a mini-seminar on diamonds. She offered to show us various stones under the microscope, explaining how each gem is unique, and how each is graded for color and brilliance. I admired a particularly beautiful stone, so she put it under the magnifying glass for me to examine. I commented on the dark lines visible under magnification.

"Oh, those are the inclusions," she said. "Every stone has its own unique inclusions along with its own unique brilliance."

"You mean flaws, right?" I asked.

She answered, "They are only flaws to those who don't understand diamonds."

Then and there God showed me a picture of how he sees each person he creates. Each one of us is a unique jewel, created to shine brilliantly in the light of God's love for us. Sure, we all have inclusions, imperfections. We live in an imperfect world. God does not intend us to be flawless in this life. Our created purpose is to let God's light shine through every facet of our being, expressing his colors and beauty through us in ways no one else can.

We can look at a diamond from one of two perspectives. If you look at a ring under the microscope every day and become intimately familiar with every flaw, you might be embarrassed by it. If you frequently compare it to a larger ring, it might appear shamefully small. You might not wear it, or you might turn it to the inside of your hand for fear that someone would notice it isn't as good as someone else's.

But that is not how God meant the beauty of diamonds to be seen. We can't appreciate the true beauty of a diamond by looking at its flaws under a microscope. Its beauty is seen when someone holds it up in the sunlight and everyone can see it sparkle. Each diamond is uniquely beautiful, a symbol of enduring love.

That is how God wants us to see ourselves and treat ourselves, as his uniquely beautiful jewels. Our attitude toward our own beauty of spirit and our imperfections will determine whether or not we shine as we were intended. We are not to misuse our time on this earth, focusing on every little flaw within us. We are created to shine with the light of God's creative genius. Each person should be appreciated as a unique part of God's masterpiece of creation, not despised as somehow inferior to someone else's attributes, talents, abilities, or situation.

Last summer, Pat and I had our fifteenth wedding anniversary. Our relationship has grown progressively better, our love stronger. We are closer now in some ways than ever before. I found that when I had to look to God to be my emotional husband for a while, it helped me overcome my fears of loving Pat again. Intimacy with God helped me rebuild intimacy with my husband. We hoped to be able to take a romantic get-away to celebrate our anniversary.

Pat secretly hoped he could afford to buy me a diamond ring to go with my wedding band. We prayed for the Lord to provide the extra money we would need for our anniversary trip. A few projects came through unexpectedly and gave us enough money for our trip and for Pat to buy me a ring. We found a diamond exactly like the one I envisioned, and he presented it to me on our anniversary. My ring is nowhere near as big as Rayna's, but that doesn't matter. I love my diamond and what it represents in terms of our marriage and my own progress toward becoming a shining one who can display God's splendor.

The fun of giving your whole life to God is giving it with abandon. You don't have to be anyone other than who he is making you to be. That is why I have been able to share my life so freely, even the imperfect parts. I have no illusions of perfection. I know my life is full of inclusions that prove to be flaws to anyone who looks closely. But I also know that God takes great delight in shining his perfect light through imperfect people. He can use whatever part of my imperfect being I surrender to him: my thoughts, my failures, my wisdom, my sorrows and joys, my humor, all my efforts, all that I am. Somehow, when I accept that he loves me, that he has honored me with his presence in my life,

I don't have to worry about people seeing the flaws. As God's light shines through my life, he changes me. While those who look for imperfection will always see it, those who have eyes to see will also see Jesus.

WHILE WAITING FOR the perfect ending, I keep a box where I collect the dreams I dare to dream. It took me many years to gather the courage to be honest about the dreams I have for my life. After losing many of my dreams, I was afraid to dream for a while. But as I stayed close to God, I sensed him encouraging me to once again begin dreaming and to pursue those dreams. I dream not only of what I want to attain, but also of who I want to become and what I want to invest to make the world a better place during my remaining time here on earth. I still keep a prayer journal where I keep track of the promises God has fulfilled and the ones I hope to see him fulfill in the future.

Last Christmas Casey wanted me to start a Bible club for her friends. I was excited that she wanted to know more about God and wanted to share this interest with her friends, but I couldn't make that commitment. Since Pat was still working a demanding, unpredictable schedule, I carried the weight of most other household responsibilities. I promised her we would start her club as soon as Pat could manage to find a job with a schedule that allowed him to take a more active role in managing our family responsibilities.

Pat and I prayed, off and on, for God to release him from his grueling schedule. He tried to arrange better hours but couldn't. He interviewed at other restaurants, but the schedules basically had the same drawbacks throughout the industry. Pat saw his job as a necessary part of the consequences from his past. He knew

God could and would release him when the time was right. I started praying for the right time to come soon, because the kids needed more time with him, and so did I.

We kept hoping that maybe I would get enough work lined up with speaking and writing so that Pat would have the financial freedom to make a transition. We agreed that if we could get ahead by a certain amount, Pat would resign his position and we would realign our family life.

Doing freelance work, I continually try to plan ahead to line up new projects before I run out of money from previous work. As I came near to completing this book, I focused on finding my next project. I had several good possibilities, but I have learned by experience that good possibilities can raise hopes that are often disappointed. It's better to not get my hopes set on any particular project until I have a contract. This time I didn't find it easy to keep from raising my hopes. I kept calculating the possibilities with one aim in mind: getting contracts in excess of the amount we agreed would be a reasonable amount to warrant Pat making a career transition.

I was scheduled to meet with my publisher in February to discuss several of these possibilities. During that trip, several projects came together. One project involves communicating the Bible to children ages seven to eleven. In meeting after meeting, everything I hoped for was realized. I sat down with my agent at the end of a long day to review the pending projects. Any way we looked at it, Pat would be able to resign. The meetings finished up on my birthday. I left the publishing offices carrying a bag of gifts and flowers from my editor. The full realization of what God had done didn't hit me until I was on the plane.

Birthdays tend to pose a challenge for me—not because I'm getting older, but because they are a time when I consider my life and my worth. Birthdays are markers. Just seven years earlier I had celebrated my birthday with fifty people. Pat had invited all the people who seemed to love me at the time, mostly people from the church where we were on staff. By my next birthday, everything had changed. I was displaced from my job. I had been in the hospital at New Life for treatment for depression, and had only just come home. A knock came at the door. There stood two of the boys from our youth group, Patrick and Chad, along with Chad's mother. One boy held a rose for me, the other held a little cake they bought at the bakery. Apart from family members who called, these three were the only ones left who remembered me on that birthday.

As I flew home on my 1995 birthday, I realized that God had given me tremendous gifts. My family was still intact. Pat, Casey, Taylor, and Haley were waiting to welcome me home. "Home" was our own home. My mom would be there too, and Papa, and the chocolate cake they baked with the kids' help. Reality began to settle in as I recounted to myself the meaning of what had just happened. Pat would finally be free to participate actively in our family again. We could go to church together as a family. I would have time available to start the Bible club for Casey and her friends. I could even use the material I would be writing for the children's project with the kids in the club.

Then it dawned on me: God had given me a job developing material for kids. He was putting me back in youth ministry, but in a way that no one could take it away from me by forcing me to resign. Even better than that, I would be ministering to my own children while I worked. Before, I had been so driven to perform that I had neglected my responsibilities at home while attempting to please people at church.

God didn't leave me in the cinders of my lost dreams. He always intended to restore what I had lost, and was doing it in a way that transformed me in the process. I looked out the window of the airplane and adjusted my hat so no one could see my tears. These were not the tears of shame or despair I cried so often over the previous years. These were tears of joy.

The prophecy was right: God had restored great joy to my life. The shakings that had come, the devastation that tried to destroy that which the Lord had done, the hurts and the scars, had all been changed. That which was a bruise had become a stone to stand upon, a declaration that would help others as they moved along. God didn't allow me to be destroyed. Instead he had built me up and increased the scope of my ministry. God was bringing me forth as a shining one, as his princess.

We refer to the day of Pat's public confession as Black Sunday. The Lord arranged for Pat's first day after he resigned from the restaurant to be Good Friday. How precious and appropriate it was for God to release him on Good Friday, the day commemorating Jesus' death on the cross.

Jesus' death on the cross makes Good Friday good because of the powerful forgiveness found in his blood—blood shed for the remission of sins. Good Friday wiped out Black Sunday when Jesus' blood wiped our sins away: Pat's, mine, the sins of those who sinned against us. The cross, a symbol of execution, became a symbol of pardon. Our family was back in church—all together   for the first time on Easter. How appropriate it seemed to us that we start the beginning of this new phase of life by celebrating Christ's resurrection (and our own).

I frequently revisit the promises written in my prayer journals. So many of them have come true in ways immeasurably more wonderful than I would have dared to ask or even think. I no longer feel disgrace; I have put the shame of my youth in the past where it belongs. I no longer feel like a widow; I feel like a bride— to Pat and to God. Though it seemed God abandoned me for a brief time, he brought me back with deep compassion. God took care of our youth group too—even the girl who collapsed at my feet. Pat sang in her wedding recently, and her faith is strong.

God promised we would receive double for all our shame. I don't know how much that is, but I know God has taken away the shame and given us far more joy instead. He bound up our wounds when we were brokenhearted. He proclaimed his favor on our lives. He freed us, released us from darkness, and took vengeance on those to whom vengeance was due. During this process, I saw God in greater dimension and found greater confidence in his steadfast love.

When I told my sister Robin all that God had done to fulfill his promises, I commented to her that God was certainly faithful.

"Yes, God is faithful," Robin responded, "but you had to remain faithful, too. Look at all the times you or Pat could have stopped following God's Word. God's faithfulness came through for you because you both chose to obey God and remain faithful to him and what you knew was right. If either of you had rebelled or given up on your faith, do you think God would do what he is doing?"

"I guess you have a point," I said.

Robin then said, "When you tell your story, tell about the faithfulness of God. But don't forget how important our faithfulness to God is too."

She was right. I had tended to focus on the faithfulness of God, if only because I was aware of my shortcomings and how weak I felt as I tried to continue dancing in the arms of God. But I chose to stay in those arms; I didn't walk away or give up on his promises. I waited to see how God could possibly get me out of a situation that seemed to have no good resolution.

All along, during the good times and times of suffering, God did his part and I did mine. He never let me go. He drew me close. His Spirit whispered that he would make my dreams come true. He provided for my needs. He healed me, restored my soul, purified me, and raised me up—not just in a fairy tale, but in real life. All of that was his part. I believed him enough to keep dancing, following his lead at every turn. That was my part, and it ultimately led to the intimacy and personal fulfillment I desired.

When I searched through my Bible, the story of Mary of Bethany seemed to illustrate perfectly what I felt the human part of the dance should be.

Before Jesus' crucifixion, he attended a dinner. During the dinner, a woman named Mary took a vial of pure nard, an expensive perfume, and broke it open. Then she poured it on Jesus' feet and wiped his feet with her hair. The house was filled with the fragrance of the perfume.

One of Jesus' disciples, Judas Iscariot, objected to Mary's act. He asked Jesus why the perfume hadn't been sold and the money given to the poor.

"'*Leave her alone*,' Jesus replied. 'It was meant that she should save this perfume for the day of my burial. You will always have the poor among you, but you will not always have me'" (John 12:7–8, italics added).

In Mark's account of the event, Jesus says, "Why are you bothering her? . . . *She did what she could.* She poured perfume on my body beforehand to prepare for my burial. I tell you the truth, wherever the gospel is preached throughout the world, what she has done will also be told, in memory of her" (Mark 14:6–9, italics added).

Mary brought her most precious treasure to pour out because of her love for Jesus. Yet when Mary poured out her treasure, she received not admiration, but criticism from those who considered themselves more practical or spiritual than she. We too can pour out that which is a precious fragrance to God: our lives. When we break our lives open and pour out the treasure of our talent, personality, and abilities, we too may be met with criticism. We must come to accept that there will always be those who consider themselves more spiritual than we are, those who point out the flaws in our offering. None of that matters.

Jesus was defending Mary when he said, "Leave her alone.... She did what she could." He knew she had done what she could to honor him and to display her love for him. She had done what she could with what she had. When we live our lives doing what we can with what we have, making the most of every opportunity, God will come to our defense. He will vindicate us before the eyes of those who misjudge us and will continue to lead us to a better life. He will honor us as he honored Mary. Our part of the dance is to do what we can and continue following his lead.

God's part in the dance is different for each person who comes to dance in his arms; he treats each one of us with respect for our uniqueness. But he is always true to his nature and true to his promises for each one of us. I see God's part of the dance in the last words of Joshua, a man who followed God his whole life, even when others turned away.

As he was dying, Joshua made a public announcement to the nation of Israel. He said, "Now I am about to go the way of all the earth. You know with all your heart and soul that not one of all the good promises the LORD your God gave you has failed. Every promise has been fulfilled; not one has failed" (Joshua 23:14).

Joshua was saying these words to those whose ancestors were born into slavery with him in Egypt. He spent forty years wandering in the wilderness with those people before leading them into the promised land. Joshua wanted to remind those he had led that God had done every single thing he planned to do in their lives.

We may have been born into slavery, but God came to free us. We may spend some time on earth wandering needlessly, but God promises to lead us to a place where we can know his love intimately, where his secure love gives us the courage to risk intimacy with others, where we can fulfill our purpose, and where our dreams can come true.

Epilogue

WHILE GOD PLAYS KEY roles in your Cinderella story, he can't be contained in these roles. He is not only the prince; he is also the kindhearted father, the fairy godmother, and the author as well! As the author and finisher of our faith, God began a good work in us and will complete it.

God is working on the story of your life. Believing this provides real hope and comfort amidst the uncertainties of life. Every good story involves a character in transformation. This transformation usually takes place in the midst of conflict: inner conflicts, conflicts with people, conflicts against forces of life and nature that threaten you. A truly great author will allow his characters to go through numerous challenges with a plan to bring about a triumph while transforming the character along the way.

Think of your life as a story in the process of being written. Be assured the author intends a happy ending, even though you will be faced with difficult challenges. The author who created you has fallen in love with you. He's not content to let you pass through the pages of one of his stories and fade from memory. You are too precious to lose. He wants you to live beyond the confines of this life—if he can be assured of your genuine love. He is trying to win your love within this story, to bring you to life after the story is over. He doesn't want to manipulate you; instead, he desires true love from the responsive heart of a woman who chooses him of her own free will.

Your life may be his ultimate adventure. He is pursuing you. You are free to choose how to respond to him, to others, and to situations he brings into your life. By giving you a free will, God has taken the ultimate risk. If you reject his love or resist becoming the woman he knows you can be, he will not force you. The choice is yours.

God takes great joy in your transformation. He loves you no less at the beginning, when you feel so unworthy, than he will when you become all he created you to be. He plans your happy ending and does his best to help you find the way. He hopes you won't make choices that bar you from the good plans he has in mind for you. He wants to show you how to overcome the villains and the challenges you must face. He longs for the day you will step out of this mortal life and into his arms in a kingdom none of us can yet fully comprehend. It is there that you can finally know him in all his fullness, know his love without limitation, and know yourself as only he knows you. That is where you will live— *happily ever after!*

Acknowledgments

MY SINCERE THANKS GO out to: Patrick Neal, my husband, for always believing in me and allowing me to share aspects of his life that he would rather not have revealed. His courage and willingness to walk in the truth made this book possible—in content, as well as in the writing.

Sealy Yates, my agent, whose integrity builds a bridge of trust so that people can come together and move forward to advance the kingdom of God. My thanks also to his staff, Susan, Tom, and Jeana, who talked me through this process.

Sandy Vander Zicht, my editor. Henry James once said, "Life is all confusion and inclusion. Art is discrimination and selection." In this respect, Sandy is an artist. I am grateful that she took the time to bring out the best in this book.

My mother, Nina Perry; and LeRoy Grant, for taking care of my children so I could finish this manuscript on time.

Gene and Jan Ebel, Bruce and Suzanne Bucholtz, for allowing me to hide away at their homes when I needed to write without interruption.

If this book raises issues or emotions that are difficult to bear alone, call New Life Clinics.
1 (800) NEW-LIFE

Connie Neal is available for a limited number of speaking engagements.
For details, call Susan Yates.
(714) 285-9540

If you received Christ for the first time through reading this book, would you please let me know? I would like to pray for you and celebrate your entrance into God's kingdom. You can send me a note via my publisher at:

Connie Neal
c/o Zondervan Publishing House
5300 Patterson Ave., S.E.
Grand Rapids, MI 49530
Attn: Author Relations

Discussion Guide

SINCE WRITING *Dancing in the Arms of God*, I've received correspondence from many women requesting a discussion guide or Bible study to accompany the book. While what you will find here is not a complete Bible study, I've provided a key Scripture passage that relates to each chapter. Those who memorize and meditate on these verses before discussing the chapter will find their discussions enriched. However, while focusing attention on God's Word will deepen your discussion and benefit those who do so, beware of making this a source of guilt for those who do not.

This book was written to meet women at various points in their relationship with God and to draw them into an intimate relationship with him. The issues touched on seem to be universal, and therefore give us a connection with others. My prayer is that women who are seeking God will feel free to join in these discussions and honestly express themselves, regardless of their religious affiliation. Your respect for each woman, regardless of where she is spiritually, and your commitment to maintain confidentiality within your group will encourage openness. Many of the questions encourage the sharing of personal experience. This is not to honor those whose relationship with God is exemplary, nor is it to outdo each other in telling our tales of woe in hopes of attracting pity. Rather, the goal is to identify where these issues connect with real life, and to lay hold of God's promises with regard to these issues. My hope is that your times of discussion will lead to times of prayer and obedience, so that you can fully experience "dancing in the arms of God."

PRELUDE

YOUR FIRST MEETING MAY be a time for making new acquaintances or for new members to see the book for the first time. Therefore, begin by reading the prelude aloud to the group, or by taking turns reading it. As the prelude is being read, identify which stanza most closely represents your current life situation and why. Take turns introducing yourselves, and sharing which stanza you chose, why you chose it, and how it relates to your current situation.

The Scripture passage that captures the overall theme for this book is Isaiah 61:1–3. Read this passage aloud from a few different Bible translations. The passage parallels the troubling situations described in the prelude: (1) being poor; (2) brokenhearted; (3) held captive; (4) in the dark; (5) in need of God's favor; (6) in need of God's vengeance on our behalf; and (7) in mourning, grief, and despair. Circle any of these that describe where you are at this season of your life. Take turns sharing what you circled.

This Scripture passage also features all the hope and promise found in the prelude: (1) One who comes to bring us good news; (2) tender care and healing for a broken heart; (3) freedom; (4) release from darkness; (5) God's favor; (6) God's promise of vengeance where it is due; (7) comfort; (8) provision; (9) a crown of beauty; (10) the oil of gladness; and (11) a garment of praise. Put a box around any of these phrases that describe what you need from God at this point in your life. Underline any that you are currently receiving from God. Take turns sharing what you boxed and what you underlined.

Prayer allows us to pour out our true feelings and real needs before God. However, effective prayer goes one step further—if it is to make a difference, we must claim the appropriate promises of God with faith. Take a few moments to pray. Using the descriptions you circled above, talk to God about your situation. Thank him for what he is currently doing according to his promise. Then ask him to provide the promises that you need in your life right now (what you boxed). Close your prayer by thanking God for his promises, his power to fulfill them, and his love for you. I suggest you keep a record of what you ask God to do in your life as you participate in this group. By the end of the book, I pray that dancing in the arms of God will not be just a concept, but a fitting description of your life.

Scripture for meditation before next meeting:
Jeremiah 29:11–13.

Chapter One

DANCING IN THE ARMS OF GOD

> *Key Point: God has wonderful plans for you. His plans unfold through relationship with him.*
> *Key Scripture Passage: Jeremiah 29:11–13*
> *Key Application Goal: Believe in God's good plans for you. Seek him with all your heart.*

1. Describe any "fairy tale hopes" you entertained as a girl. How have these been realized or disappointed?
2. How do you relate to the picture of a little girl sitting on a garbage can? What kind of "garbage" has surrounded your life?
3. How have you seen God lift you up from the garbage?
4. I shared my experience of being introduced to Jesus Christ and accepting his offer of love. Can you recall the moment you chose to accept God's offer of love in Jesus Christ?
5. Dancing in the arms of God describes a relationship between you and God that makes a real difference in your life. How has your relationship with God been demonstrated in your life?
6. Dancing in the arms of God represents partnering with God in an intimate and loving way. Have you previously pictured your relationship with God differently? (Father to child, Judge to penitent sinner, Master to servant) How does thinking of God in terms of love and intimacy stretch your view of God and your relationship with him?

Scripture for meditation before next meeting:
Psalm 146:3–8

Chapter Two

SOMEDAY MY PRINCE WILL COME

Key Point: God is faithful—even when people fail you.
Key Scripture Passage: Psalm 146:3–8
Key Application Goal: Put your trust fully in God!

1. When have you engaged in fantasies that someday your prince would come to your rescue? To what degree did these fantasies lead to fulfillment or to disillusionment?

2. How have disappointments in relationships with men influenced your view of God? (Who the Bible reveals in masculine terms as Father, Brother, and Son of Man)

3. God is "enthralled by your beauty." Can you accept this as God's view of you? If not, what keeps you from believing this? How might your self-image and your life be different if you believed this?

4. When we've been hurt or disappointed in relationships with men, we tend to look elsewhere to fill the void and heal the hurt. Have you experienced this? If so, how have you sought to fill this inner void? What level of satisfaction have your efforts brought you?

5. When we seek to fill our inner void apart from God, we tend to become obsessive or excessive in our pursuit of the love we need. When have you become excessive or obsessive in trying to get the love you needed? Did you disobey God's commands in the process? What was the outcome of these pursuits?

6. The chapter stated, "Our desires for fulfillment, acceptance, unconditional love, security, and validation are good. We need only transfer them to the one capable of fulfilling them." How do you transfer these real needs to God in real ways? How does this impact your relationships with God and people?

7. Looking to God as our ultimate fulfillment and allowing his love to fill the voids in our lives should help us build healthier relationships with men. Read 1 John 4:19–21. How has your relationship with God influenced your relationships with men in a positive way?

Scripture for Meditation before next meeting:
Lamentations 3:16–26

Chapter Three

LIFE AMIDST THE ASHES

> *Key Point: God's compassion never runs out.*
> *Key Scripture Passage: Lamentations 3:16–26*
> *Key Application Goal: Don't give up. When all you hoped for is gone—hope in God!*

1. Cinder-Ella took her identity from the cinders in which she sat. How do the cinders of your life mar your God-given identity?

2. Our response to God in the midst of fiery trials determines whether or not the fires purify our faith. What fiery trials have purified your faith?

3. Look at the list that describes living amidst the cinders. Do any of these describe you? If so, which ones? What will you do to allow God to turn your cinders into ashes?

4. Look at the list for living amidst the ashes. Which of these are you willing to do? Which will require God's miraculous power?

5. Five steps are given to help you move from cinders to the ashes. Which of these have you already done, and how? Which have you neglected or refused to do, and why?

Scripture for Meditation before next meeting:
Galatians 4:1–7

Chapter Four

Everybody's Servant

> *Key Point: You're not a slave anymore; you're an heir of God.*
>
> *Key Scripture Passage: Galatians 4:1–7*
>
> *Key Application Goal: Don't keep living like a slave when you don't have to!*

1. In what ways do you feel like you have to earn your keep? How does this affect you at home, work, church, and in your community?

2. If you've put your faith in Jesus Christ, God has freed you from slavery and elevated you to the position of royal heir. How do you act like a slave who has to work tirelessly to retain God's favor? How do you act like a royal heir?

3. "God doesn't want our performance; he wants us. He doesn't demand our perfection; he gives us his." Do you believe this? How does (or would) believing this free you to do things that you may be afraid to do while trying to please people?

4. At one point in my life, I began to play at life, secure in the knowledge that there was no way I could lose God's love. Do you feel the freedom to play at life? On a scale of 1 to 10 (1= not sure, 10= absolutely certain), how sure are you that you cannot lose God's love?

5. In the illustration of Timmy eating Taylor's artwork, Taylor looked to Timmy for affirmation and was devastated when he didn't get it. To whom have you looked for affirmation? How have you been impacted by not receiving the affirmation you sought? How has this inhibited your self-expression? Given that God treasures your "artwork," how can you begin to express yourself and your talents without reservation?

6. When—if ever—have you come to realize that God loves you for who you are not just what you do? If you've had this experience, describe how it affected you.

Scripture for Meditation before next meeting:
Romans 8:31–39

Chapter Five

THE SEARCH FOR TRUE LOVE

Key Point: You are loved!
Key Scripture Passage: Romans 8:31–39
*Key Application Goal: Live like you are loved—and
can never be unloved.*

1. How does the prince, disguising himself as a commoner, add depth to the love story? How does realizing that Jesus left the glory of heaven to seek your love add depth to your relationship with him?

2. In what ways do you relate to the woman Jesus met at the well? How are you like and unlike her? What do you think it means to worship in spirit and in truth?

3. Cinderella ran away out of fear that her shame would be revealed. When have you run away from God or people because you feared your shame would be exposed? When Jesus died he bore our shame. How might this realization help you turn toward God rather than turning away when you feel ashamed?

4. The illustration of Pat's secret life shows how a person can cut himself off from receiving love. Are there secrets you harbor because you believe that someone would not love you if they knew the "real" you? Read James 5:16. What words of encouragement do you have for anyone in your group who might be afraid to confess some dark secret for fear of being rejected? How can God help us receive true love through our human relationships?

5. I shared specific moments when Maya Angelou and I realized the truth of God's love. When can you recall realizing that God loves you?

6. Edith's story shows that true love is more about self-sacrifice and devotion than glamour. How does this story encourage or inspire you?

Scripture for Meditation before next meeting:
Isaiah 55:1–7

Chapter Six

ALL THE ELIGIBLE MAIDENS

> *Key Point: You're invited to God's banquet.*
> *Key Scripture Passage: Isaiah 55:1–7*
> *Key Application Goal: Accept God's invitation and celebrate life!*

1. Who has played the role of a "wicked stepsister" in your life? What has this person pointed to in an attempt to disqualify you from the abundant life God has for you?

2. This chapter asserts, "The surest way to miss the ball is to believe that we are not one of the eligible maidens. Then we may give up seeking our dreams. What has caused you to see yourself as ineligible and to relinquish your hopes and dreams?

3. This chapter describes the difference between one who believes those who say she's not eligible and the one who believes God's voice saying that she is. Who do you tend to believe? How does believing what God says about you help you? In what ways does believing the negative voices of others keep you from fulfilling God's dreams for you and your heart's desires?

4. Many women are so busy doing what has to be done that they make no time to pursue their dreams or develop their talents. What, if anything, gets in your way? If you had the time, what talents would you develop or what dream would you pursue? Are you willing to make a little time to develop your talents and pursue your dreams?

5. God has a noble purpose for our lives. This chapter describes several ways you can prepare yourself to fulfill your purpose. The following questions will help you identify how well you're doing:

- How are you making the most of opportunities where you are, doing what you are doing, to make a positive impact?
- How are you working to develop your talents, skills, and abilities?
- How are you educating yourself to provide a useful service?
- Describe a time when you were criticized and sorted out the useful truth from the destructive trash. Or share a time when criticism hindered you. See if the group can help you sort out any useful bits of truth and discard the rest.
- How have you been working hard to persevere in these pursuits?

Scripture for Meditation before next meeting:
Romans 12:1–2

Chapter Seven

DRY YOUR EYES, YOU CAN'T GO TO THE BALL LOOKING LIKE THAT!

Key Point: If you're not satisfied with yourself, don't worry. You can change!
Key Scripture Passage: Romans 12:1–2
Key Application Goal: Give yourself completely to God; then be transformed by the renewing of your mind.

1. In what ways have you tried to make yourself over in an attempt to be accepted?
2. How do you need to change if your dreams are to come true? How have you tried and failed to make these changes before?

3. In the illustration of crossing the frozen river, it was the strength of that in which each woman placed her faith that mattered most. How can you depend more upon God's strength and less on your own?

4. Read Psalm 37:4. How are you delighting yourself in God? What desires are in your heart? Take a moment to ask God to bring them to pass.

5. The story of praying for my mom shows how scary it can be to trust God to transform our loved ones. How has fear of disappointment kept you from praying for someone you love?

6. Which of the principles of transformation in this chapter are operating in your life?

Scripture for Meditation before next meeting:
Psalm 45:10–15

Chapter Eight

God Desires Your Beauty

> *Key Point: God created beauty within you. Allow God to bring out your true beauty!*
> *Key Scripture Passage: Psalm 45:10–15*
> *Key Application Goal: Believe God's view of you. Nurture yourself to bring out your beauty.*

1. In what ways might you be living out your days "in the dirty rags that characterize your past?"

2. When you see aspects of yourself that don't appear beautiful, how are you most inclined to react: with anger, by hiding yourself away in shame, or by trying to cover up the "ugliness" with outward adornments?

3. In this chapter, I suggest four things you can do to acknowledge and bring out the beauty within you. Which of these have you done and to what effect? Which haven't you done and why not?

4. In our society, people's attitudes change toward others based on physical appearance. How has this impacted your self-image? How has this kind of bias influenced your opinion of, or relationship with, others? Since God looks on the heart, how should your relationship with God change your view and treatment of people who don't measure up to society's standards of beauty? How has your relationship with God changed how you view and treat others?

5. God didn't just change my view of myself, he intervened to change my life. How has God intervened in your life in tangible ways?

6. In what specific ways do you see beauty in the other members of your group (that they may be blind to in themselves)?

**Scripture for Meditation before next meeting:
Philippians 3:7–11**

Chapter Nine

GLASS SLIPPERS AND OTHER LOST TREASURES

Key Point: Your losses can lead to great gain.
Key Scripture Passage: Philippians 3:7–11
Key Application Goal: Leave your losses in God's hands
willingly. Trust him with them.

1. Given the analogy I used, what does Cinderella's lost glass slipper represent in your life? What dreams that held promise have been lost to you? How have you let go? Or how are you still trying to hold on to a dream that is slipping away?

2. In times of loss, how have you experienced the assurance that "God picks up our lost treasures and holds them dear to his heart?" When have you seen God's faithfulness in someone else's life? How did this impact your faith?

3. How might God transform your losses so that you can help others who are hurting? Who can you encourage because of what you've been through?

4. How has turning to God in times of loss and grief helped you? How has turning away from God during such times impacted your life? What do you make of Jesus' words, "Blessed are those who mourn, for they will be comforted," found in Matt. 5:4?

5. In times of grief Jeremiah called to mind God's compassion and spoke to himself the words recorded in Lamentations 3:26. This gave him hope. In times of grief, what do you call to mind? How is your choice of thoughts and self-talk different from or similar to Jeremiah's? What influence does your choice of thoughts and self-talk have on your level of hope?

6. God may test our faith by asking us to sacrifice that which we hold dear in order to give us something far better. What have you sacrificed or released to God that led ultimately to something better?

7. How have you seen God use a loss (yours or another's) to do something immeasurably more than anything you could ask or imagine?

Scripture for Meditation before next meeting:
Luke 9:59–62

Chapter Ten

AT THE STROKE OF MIDNIGHT

*Key Point: Jesus doesn't force anyone to follow him —
ever. It's your choice.*

Key Scripture Passage: Luke 9:59–62
Key Application Goal: Don't let anything distract you
from following Jesus.

1. When has disillusionment threatened your relationship with God?

2. Where do you turn for assurance that God loves you—even when all seems dark and God seems distant?

3. During times of disillusionment we need to cling to God's Word, especially to his promises that apply to our lives. Which of the Scriptures cited in this chapter are of particular encouragement to you? Why? What other promises from God's Word do you rely on when you are disillusioned? Can you cite a passage of Scripture you memorized that has given you strength in time of need?

4. How solid is your reasoned understanding of why you believe the Bible and Jesus' teachings? If your intellectual confidence is shaky, what will you do to develop it?

5. How have you commemorated the promises God has fulfilled in your life?

6. Jesus promised we would all face trouble in this life. How has knowing or not knowing this affected your faith when troubles came?

7. How have your temptations been heightened during times of trouble? What is the source of any bitterness within you? How does bitterness and unresolved anger toward God and others make you more susceptible when you are tempted?

8. What legitimate needs in your life—for love, approval, acceptance, belonging, and so on—are going unmet? What role does fear play in keeping you from meeting these needs in ways God approves? How are you tempted to meet these needs in ungodly ways?

Scripture for Meditation before next meeting:
Proverbs 31:25–31

Chapter Eleven

THE STRENGTH AND DIGNITY OF THE PRINCESS BRIDE

Key Point: We are called to conduct ourselves in a manner fitting a princess in God's kingdom.
Key Scripture Passage: Proverbs 31:25–31
Key Application Goal: Respect your position, understand your privileges, and use your power wisely.

1. How have you internalized God's view of you as his Princess Bride? How does realizing God's love for you influence your self-respect?

2. When have you realized that you were caught in a conflict between the kingdom of God and spiritual forces of wickedness? Were you prepared to stand firm in your faith? We are to put on the full armor of God. How do you do this in everyday life?

3. When people put you down and don't treat you with respect, how do you show self-respect? What difference does this make?

4. Spiritual kingdoms and spheres of influence are real. Those who serve in them do so to real effect. How do you help establish and advance God's kingdom?

5. Refer to the list of privileges of the Princess Bride. How do you use these to good effect for the kingdom of God and for your life?

6. In what situations do you tend to act in a less than dignified way? How could what you learned in this chapter help you respond with strength and dignity the next time you are in such a situation?

Scripture for Meditation before next meeting:
John 14:1–6

Chapter Twelve

UNTIL HAPPILY EVER AFTER . . .

> *Key Point: Your life story is just a prelude to the eternal life.*
> *Key Scripture Passage: John 14:1–6*
> *Key Application Goal: Live your life here and now, in light of eternity.*

1. While we can't live happily ever after in this world, we can thank God for the happiness we enjoy. What happiness do you enjoy? When do you thank God for supplying this happiness?

2. In what situations have you dared to hope for beauty instead of ashes, gladness instead of mourning, and praise instead of despair?

3. Refer to the illustration from *Mirette on the High Wire.* To what do you aspire? What requires perseverence? What responsibilities and aspirations require your focused attention? How are you balancing your responsibilities with the pursuit of your aspirations? Do you need to eliminate some activities, commitments, or distractions so that you can balance your life? If so, what needs to go?

4. How can you use your past mistakes to redirect your future in the direction of your dreams and God's dreams for you?

5. Think of yourself as God's jewel. What flaws do you focus on? Describe a time when you have chosen to accept your flaws and let the light of God shine through every unique facet of your being. How does your choice of perspective influence your life?

6. God's part in the dance is to fulfill his promises to us faithfully. What promises have you seen God fulfill already? What promises are you still waiting for God to fulfill that require your ongoing faith and patience?

7. Our part is to devote our lives to God, do what we can, and continue following his lead. How are you doing on your part of the dance? In what areas can you do better?

EPILOGUE

1. The epilogue says that God is the author of your story, in search of a happy ending for your life. How does this view of God's involvement in your life change your outlook?

2. If your life is like God's love story in which he is pursuing you to become his bride, you will either accept or refuse his overtures of love. John 3:16 says, "For God so loved the world that he gave his one and only Son, that whoever believes in him shall not perish but have eternal life." God loves all the eligible maidens. All are invited into his kingdom, but only those who accept his invitation will enter in. John 1:12 says, "Yet to all who received him, to those who believed in his name, he gave the right to become children of God . . ." If you have not received Jesus Christ as your Savior and Lord, will you now? He has offered you a proposal and paid your dowry with his blood.

Dear Jesus,

Thank you for coming to earth in search of a bride.

Thank you for living a sinless life to provide robes of righteousness to cover my shame.

I know that I am a sinner, unworthy—and yet accepted by you.

I put my faith in you. I accept your offer of forgiveness and love.

Please accept me into your kingdom.

Please teach me to obey you and to live my life dancing in your arms.

AMEN!